Praise for
10 Ultimate Truths Girls Should Know

"Every young girl needs to read this book! But then again, these *10 ultimate truths* aren't just for girls! As the mother of three boys, I'm so thankful for the wisdom packed into this book that I know will greatly benefit my boys. Kari isn't afraid to tackle our kids' toughest challenges, and she does so with extraordinary grace and profound Biblical truth. I wish this book had been available when I was young!"

JEANNIE CUNNION, MSW, AUTHOR OF *PARENTING THE WHOLEHEARTED CHILD*

"Kari delves straight into the mind of today's teen and speaks truth into her soul. In *10 Ultimate Truths Girls Should Know*, Kari equips girls with a spiritual roadmap to help navigate through the transitional years into womanhood. The relevant and engaging topics make *10 Ultimate Truths Girls Should Know* an ideal choice for small-group discussion."

ALLISON HENDRIX—WRITER, THE HOUSE OF HENDRIX BLOG

"Kari presents for her readers a dynamic and challenging book. God calls each of us to be the 'best version of ourselves.' Kari presents to her readers a roadmap for that journey, for there can be no authentic spirituality without authentic development. Kari reminds us that we need to assess where we are in order to see where we need to grow and then to commit ourselves to take steps needed for development and continuous growth. Girls are reminded to see their relationship with God, themselves, and others as integral to their physical and spiritual development."

REVEREND ROBERT J. SULLIVAN, ST. FRANCIS XAVIER
CATHOLIC CHURCH, BIRMINGHAM, ALABAMA

"Girls are wonderful! Girls are complicated! They are God's special creation made specifically to bring honor and glory to Him. Kari Kampakis has so beautifully set forth TRUTH through stories and Scripture. Her wisdom and insight reach to the depths of the heart of adolescent young ladies. Each principle and chapter leads the reader to ponder her own identity with the hopes that she will more and more realize how deeply loved she is by Christ, and by accepting that love, the girl will be on her way to becoming the beautiful person God created her to be. This is a wonderful tool for students, youth leaders, and parents."

DONNA GREENE, FOUNDER AND DIRECTOR, COMMUNITY MINISTRY FOR GIRLS, INC., AND AUTHOR OF *GROWING GODLY WOMEN*, *LETTERS FROM CAMPUS*, *TWENTYSOMETHING GIRL*, *TO KNOT OR NOT*, *CELEBRATE IN SPITE OF CANCER*, AND *FOR NATALEE . . . A COMMUNITY OF LOVE*.

"This book is more than good advice. Rather, it is a journey for parents and daughters, indeed women of any age, through the minefields of childhood and adolescence, all guided by the timeless Truth of Jesus. Read this book, and share."

THE REVEREND RICHMOND WEBSTER, SAINT LUKE'S EPISCOPAL CHURCH, BIRMINGHAM, ALABAMA

"This is an excellent book! It provides great wisdom for young women who are growing up and trying to figure out how to live in this secular age. It is a great read!"

RICHARD SIMMONS III, EXECUTIVE DIRECTOR, THE CENTER FOR EXECUTIVE LEADERSHIP, AND ALSO AN AUTHOR OF FIVE BOOKS

"Kari Kampakis writes with a warrior's passion on a mission to capture young girls' hearts. The best part of *10 Ultimate Truths Girls Should Know* is the reading connects with females of all ages. Kari uses practical remedies to not only ease the pain of these tumultuous years, but maybe even avoid the circumstances entirely. *10 Ultimate Truths Girls Should Know* is a must-read for women of all ages, but most importantly a necessity for mothers and their daughters."

CHRISTY K. TRUITT IS AN AWARD-WINNING WRITER OF SOUTHERN FICTION. HER LATEST NOVEL, *THE FIRST DROP OF RAIN*, RELEASES FALL 2014.

10 Ultimate Truths Girls Should Know

KARI KAMPAKIS

THOMAS NELSON
Since 1798

NASHVILLE MEXICO CITY RIO DE JANEIRO

Published in Nashville, Tennessee, by Thomas Nelson. Thomas Nelson is a registered trademark of HarperCollins Christian Publishing, Inc.

Thomas Nelson titles may be purchased in bulk for educational, business, fund-raising, or sales promotional use. For information, please e-mail SpecialMarkets@ ThomasNelson.com.

Unless otherwise noted, Scripture quotations are taken from THE HOLY BIBLE, NEW INTERNATIONAL VERSION®, NIV®. Copyright © 1973, 1978, 1984, 2011 by Biblica, Inc.™ Used by permission. All rights reserved worldwide.

Scripture quotations marked NLT are taken from *Holy Bible*, New Living Translation. © 1996. Used by permission of Tyndale House Publishers, Inc., Wheaton, Illinois 60189. All rights reserved.

Scripture quotations marked ESV are taken from THE ENGLISH STANDARD VERSION. © 2001 by Crossway Bibles, a division of Good News Publishers. Used by permission.

Scripture quotations marked CEV are taken from THE CONTEMPORARY ENGLISH VERSION. © 1991 by the American Bible Society. Used by permission.

Library of Congress Cataloging-in-Publication Data

Kampakis, Kari, 1972– author.
10 ultimate truths girls should know / Kari Kampakis.
    pages cm
Audience: Age 12-16.
Includes bibliographical references.
ISBN 978-0-529-11103-6 (softcover) -- ISBN 0-529-11103-9 (softcover) 1. Teenage girls--Religious life--Juvenile literature. 2. Teenage girls--Conduct of life--Juvenile literature. 3. Christian life--Biblical teaching--Juvenile literature. I. Title. II. Title: Ten ultimate truths girls should know.
BV4551.3.K36 2014
248.8'33--dc23

                                        2014031320

Printed in the United States

16 17 18 RRD 12 11 10 9 8

To Mom and Dad, for modeling God's love
every day of my life. I love you both.

To Harry, my soul mate and best friend, whose love,
humility, and patience help me understand Christ better.
I love you, and I'm thankful to be your wife.

And to my daughters: Ella, Sophie, Marie Claire, and Camille.
You girls are my angels, living reminders that there is, indeed,
a heaven. This book is for you, written as encouragement
for the road ahead. Be bold and brave as you serve God,
remembering that whatever happens, I'll always love you.

Contents

The 10 Ultimate Truths

Truth #10: KINDNESS is more important than POPULARITY.

Truth #9: You were born to fly.

Truth #8: Today's choices set the stage for your reputation.

Truth #7: Chasing boys doesn't make you cool. It makes you a nuisance.

Truth #6: You weren't made to worship yourself.

Truth #5: People peak at different times in life. Trust God's plan for you.

Truth #4: Get comfortable with being uncomfortable. Otherwise you'll never stick to your guns.

Truth #3: Boys are visual creatures. The clothing choices you make affect the way they see you.

Truth #2: Pretty girls are a dime a dozen. Outer beauty attracts attention, but inner beauty is what holds it.

Truth #1: The source of all peace and happiness lives inside you. Learn to listen to the whispers of God over the megaphone of public opinion.

Introduction

> Is it joy you want? What if I told you about a joy that longs to wrap its arms around you, hold you close, and tell you how unconditionally loved you are?

here are two things no one can prepare you for.

One is how *fun* it is to be a girl.

The other is how *hard* it is to be a girl.

Let's start with the fun side. Isn't it great to be part of the gender that finds it perfectly acceptable to sing at the top of your lungs, dance in the kitchen, and jump up and down squealing with your best friend because you both bought the same bathing suit?

What about slumber parties, girls' nights, and deep conversations in the dark, where you pour out your heart until three o'clock in the morning? Can you even *imagine* life without these joys?

On the flip side, there is a dark underbelly to being female that makes some days tough. The mean girls who criticize your singing and dancing, for instance. The best friend who accuses you of copying her when you show up in the same bathing suit. The slumber parties you aren't invited to. The girls' night that leads to drama. The secrets you share with a trusted soul on Saturday night—only to have them broadcast at school Monday morning.

If only life could be consistent.

If only bad days weren't so bad.

If only you knew, beyond a doubt, that all your joy and pain would amount to something.

If only.

My friend, I don't know which way your life is swaying right now, whether you're living the dream or gasping for air, but either way, I have some truths to center you. As everything changes around you and inside you—your feelings, your friends, your body, your circumstances—you can cling to these truths like a ten-ton boulder.

The God who made you loves you passionately.

He created you in His image to serve your generation like no one in the universe has ever served before.

His plans for your future would astonish you. You can anticipate them with great expectation.

Now, I'm not promising that your life will be a cakewalk. I'm not touting God as a magic genie who will make all your wishes come true, from winning the Olympics to becoming an international rock star.

What I'm saying is that your Maker is your biggest fan. He thinks about you constantly and loves you more than your parents and anyone else on earth. *God created you for a purpose, and when you discover His purpose for you, you live your best life possible.*

You find peace.

You find security.

You find love, joy, courage, confidence, acceptance, and an unimaginable strength that equips you to handle any curveball you face.

So how do you start? How do you find God's designated path for you? Can you rely on your feelings and emotions to always point you in the right direction?

Your feelings and emotions are very important. They're part of the inner radar that helps guide you. (Think of a time when someone gave you a funny feeling, and you found out later how your suspicions were correct. When a situation doesn't feel or seem right—well, it probably isn't right.) But sometimes feelings and emotions can blur your thinking. Sometimes they put thoughts in your head that simply aren't true.

While you may *feel* invisible in a crowd, you aren't invisible to God.

While you may *feel* forgotten by the world, you aren't forgotten by God.

While you may *feel* your future is hopeless, you always have hope through God.

Feelings and emotions swing like the weather—they can be sunny one day, cloudy the next. They're up, down, and all around. That's why you need something bigger to base your life upon and steadier to test your feelings and emotions against.

This is where the truth comes in.

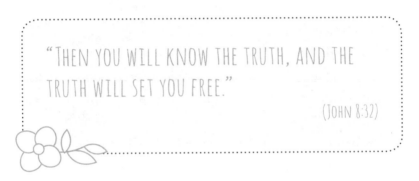

"THEN YOU WILL KNOW THE TRUTH, AND THE TRUTH WILL SET YOU FREE."

(JOHN 8:32)

WHY THE TRUTH MATTERS

Has anyone ever lied to you?

Have you ever been blindsided by a person you trusted?

If so, how did you feel afterward? How did the event change you or that relationship?

At some point, we all get hurt by lies. We all encounter dishonesty. And while the experience can be heart-wrenching, you get past the pain. You learn from it and also learn to trust your gut instincts that suggest signs of trouble early on.

Deep down, we all crave the truth. And if there's a silver

lining to being fed lies, it's the fact that deceit can trigger your hunger for the truth. Because once you get duped or betrayed, you lose tolerance for lies. You gain a stronger desire for a life that is real, meaningful, and honest.

This puts you on a better path because a quest for the truth is a quest for God. Since God *is* truth, you can't separate the two. Where one exists, you find the other.

God knows the truth isn't always obvious and clear, however. He understands what you're up against in the pressures and temptations you face, and He hears those questions stirring up confusion in your head. Because He loves you, God gives you a lamp for your journey: *His Son, Jesus Christ, a light to follow to help you navigate our broken and sometimes dark world.*

Jesus is the Way, the Truth, and the Life. No one comes to the Father except through Him (John 14:6). Throughout the Bible, God makes it clear that a relationship with Jesus is crucial to salvation. Jesus is your bridge to heaven and my bridge too. Only He can lead us to eternal life.

The 10 Ultimate Truths are designed to point you to Jesus. Through real and fictional stories, I illustrate principles you can apply to your life. Where you are now is a somewhat tricky stage. Doing the right thing isn't always socially acceptable, is it? It may cramp your social life. It may get you excluded from cool parties. You might be labeled a "goody-goody" or wonder what's wrong with you because you can't in good conscience push limits like some of your peers.

Or maybe you do push limits . . . but it unsettles you. You

think it's too late to change because God wouldn't want to associate with someone like you. If that's the case, remember this: *we're all sinners saved by God's grace.* He loves you just as much as the saints who walked this earth. And if there's a breath left in you, God can use you for His kingdom (Ephesians 4:11–13). He can renew your heart, mind, and spirit.

Whether your life's been terrific or challenging, the truth makes it *better.* What no eye has seen, what no ear has heard, and what no human mind has conceived, God has prepared for those who love him (1 Corinthians 2:9). *The purpose of life is to know, love, and serve the Lord.* And when you invite Jesus into your heart, He amplifies your joy, eases your pain, and helps you see the good work God is already doing in your life so you can share the good news with others.

Whatever you're dreaming for yourself, God's vision is bigger. Just thinking about the blessings still ahead for you floods my heart with happiness. The best is yet to come, my friend. Set your eyes on Jesus and the truth, and He'll lead you to the ultimate reward.

Your sister in Christ,

Kari

Chapter 1

Popularity

Truth #10: KINDNESS is more important than POPULARITY.

Sadie knew how mean her friend Abbie could be, but since Abbie rarely turned that meanness on her, it wasn't a big deal.

In many ways Sadie liked having a strong, bold friend like Abbie because it made her strong and bold too. It also protected Sadie. At their school there was a lot of bullying, but no one messed with The Queens—their group of friends—because messing with a Queen was messing with Abbie, and anyone who knew *anything* knew that was a mistake.

During lunch one day, Abbie announced a game she wanted to try.

"I have a great idea," she said, her face glowing. "Every week, we're going to leave out a different Queen. I decide who, and you can't talk to anyone in the group, sit with us, or make eye contact. You can't talk to anyone else either, because the point is to look like a loser so we can laugh at you. It's all a joke, so no getting mad."

Abbie locked eyes with every Queen at the cafeteria table. Apparently, being in her circle wasn't so safe after all. "Okay?" Abbie asked. "Everyone in?"

Sadie thought this was the dumbest idea ever. It really made no sense. But like the other five girls, she nodded, because when Abbie spoke, a nod was always an appropriate answer.

"Fantastic." Abbie grinned. "Let's start. Who will be the lucky girl this week?" She glanced around and stopped at Sadie. "You. Get up."

"Me?" Sadie was shocked.

"Yes, *you*." Abbie pointed at an empty table nearby. "Sit over there."

"But why?" Sadie felt a little sick. She and Abbie had been friends since birth. Their moms were college roommates. They'd taken dance together for three years. What was the point of this? For some reason she couldn't explain, Sadie's eyes began to water. Abbie was quick to notice.

"Are you *crying*?" Abbie laughed and looked at the other Queens to see who else thought this was funny. "I swear you're such a baby sometimes. It's just a game. Toughen up."

Sadie wiped her eyes. She forbade herself to cry any more

tears. "I don't want to sit by myself," she replied, holding her chin up.

"Too bad"—Abbie leaned in and narrowed her eyes on Sadie—"*you don't make the rules.* Now get going and do what I say. I'm going to take your lonely picture and post it all over the Internet. I bet I'll get two hundred likes!"

Sadie hated when Abbie got bossy. Why did *she* always call the shots? Why did no one ever challenge her? Sadie hoped that another Queen might stick up for her, but no one did. They were probably too relieved that Abbie hadn't chosen them.

Seeing no other option, Sadie walked to the empty table. There were ten seats on each side, and she sat in the middle. Sadie heard the Queens giggle, and when she looked up, they snapped her picture with their cell phones. Not only was Sadie embarrassed, she was mad—mad at them and mad at herself for going along with this.

Why did she let Abbie rule her life? Why did she give her that power?

Deep down, Sadie knew why. To be a Queen and enjoy popularity, you *had* to follow Abbie. There was no way around it. Plus, Abbie could be really fun sometimes. She organized great parties and made a big fuss over everyone's birthday. When she wasn't making life miserable for someone, Abbie could be sweet.

"You mind if I sit here?" a voice said. Sadie looked up and saw Krissie Pratt, the school's star tennis player, standing across from her with a lunch tray. Sadie had never talked to

Krissie, and all she really knew about her was that she'd raised $50,000 for Children's Hospital last year through a tennis tournament fund-raiser.

The Queens weren't supposed to associate with outsiders. But since Sadie was in a defiant mood, she did the unthinkable.

She let Krissie sit down.

Her intention was to spite Abbie, but as Krissie began talking, Sadie realized how much she *liked* her. Krissie was real and funny. Not rude-funny like Abbie, who made jokes at people's expense, but funny in her perspective. When Krissie described how her brother's iguana escaped from his cage the night before and snuck into her bed, Sadie nearly choked on her turkey sandwich. She hadn't laughed that hard in a long time.

On the table, Sadie's cell phone buzzed. Abbie had sent three texts.

Text 1: *You're laughing???*

Text 2: *You broke a rule.*

Text 3: *We'll now ignore you for TWO WEEKS!*

When Sadie looked up, Abbie smiled smugly. It gave Abbie tremendous pleasure to get in the last word. In that moment, Sadie made a choice. It was a big one too. She was *done* with Abbie, *done* with The Queens, *done* with the kissing up. It was an exhausting way to live, and for what? What did those girls give her besides constant insecurity?

From now on, Sadie wanted friends like Krissie. She wanted to spend time with people who made her laugh until her stomach hurt and would never force her to sit by herself so they could post her lonely picture all over the Internet.

"WHAT, THEN, SHALL WE SAY IN RESPONSE TO THESE THINGS? IF GOD IS FOR US, WHO CAN BE AGAINST US?"

(ROMANS 8:31)

WHY ARE MEAN GIRLS POPULAR?

Chances are, you've met some Abbies in your life.

Or maybe you are an Abbie, the ringleader everyone worships.

Either way, I'd like to share some thoughts about the social scene you're currently in and how it *will* evolve over time.

Generally speaking, girls want to be popular. Popularity *is* the Holy Grail, what the vast majority of girls compete for. With only a few coveted spots at the top, it can get ugly. Oftentimes, girls will turn on each other and use each other to gain popularity. They'll trade in their values and virtues for pride and selfish ambition.

In some classes, the most popular girls are kind. They may be the cheerleaders with a tight-knit circle, but they're nice. They set a bar of kindness at the top that trickles down and sets the tone for everyone. If you're in a class where kindness is the norm, consider yourself lucky. Not everyone is so fortunate.

Because far too often, the most popular girls are mean. They run the show like Abbie, and since everyone is scared of them, they rarely get challenged. When you see a class that tolerates a lot of cruelty, look at the top of the social food chain. Chances are, the bullies call the shots.

What you should know is this: *The mean girls are a minority that feels like a majority. They're a small core of the population that seems big due to its power and influence.*

Who gives mean girls their power? Their followers—the girls (and guys) who tag along and tell them how great they are, sacrificing their own voices and losing their identities to be in the cool circle. Without a posse, mean girls are powerless. They have no hedge to protect them, no one to cover up the big truth lurking behind the scenes; they're just as insecure and ordinary as anyone else.

Why would anyone follow a mean girl? Typically it's not because they like her. The most likely reasons are listed below:

- They want to be popular—and popularity by association works fine
- They crave security (not knowing it's false security they get)
- They want to stay on her good side

- They're unaware that better friends exist
- They're using the mean girl for personal motives
- They're scared to leave

You know in *The Wizard of Oz* when the curtain gets pulled back, and the Great and Powerful Oz is revealed as an ordinary man,[1] not the image in front of the curtain? *Mean girls live in fear of moments like that.* They know they're frauds, less powerful than people think, and to be exposed would be their ultimate humiliation.

It takes time, but girls who act mean inevitably get what they have coming. Eventually they fall from grace as their peers wise up, get a spine, and stop bowing down to them. If you're in a mean girl's circle, you'll go down too. Don't expect your friendships to resurrect themselves either, because they were a house of cards to begin with, too fragile to last.

You want to put the mean girls out of business? Then band together as much kindness as you possibly can. Show the power of *real friendships* and *good intentions*. Stand up for anyone being taunted or bullied. Love is a universal language, and when you base an alliance on that, it attracts people. You gain strength and a solid foundation to build friendships upon.

Mean girls lose power when their followers jump ship. And since their followers are often like Sadie—blindly obeying—they may have to get burned before pulling back and considering alternatives. Some girls never learn, but many do. They meet someone like Krissie and realize what they're missing. Once they recognize true friendship, they don't want to settle for a phony substitute.

We all have some *mean girl* in us, and certainly mean moments, but most people want to do the right thing. Most people want friendships where you celebrate each other instead of tear each other down. Being mean may give you a place in the popular crowd, but it won't endear you to anyone. And since popularity is a moving target, always subject to change, there's less security than you think.

The happiest, healthiest friendships are based on love—not love for yourself, but love for your friend.

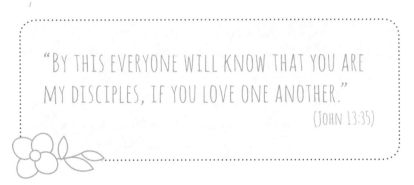

"BY THIS EVERYONE WILL KNOW THAT YOU ARE MY DISCIPLES, IF YOU LOVE ONE ANOTHER."
(JOHN 13:35)

WHY DO FRIENDS HURT FRIENDS?

I hear so many stories of girls being mean, and they all break my heart.

But the worst stories are those where friends turn on friends. It's one thing when an acquaintance attacks you—but quite another when a friend does.

The people you're closest to have the most potential to hurt you. Yes, they know your private life details, but more importantly, you trust them. You value their opinions and care what they think. So when they betray you, or you betray them, it's a dagger to the heart.

Imagine scrolling through your social media news feed and seeing that your "best friends" have posted an unflattering picture of you captioned *Loser*. They're mad because you left them for three weeks to attend summer camp. On top of that, you made new friends. The nerve! They all agreed you deserve payback, and now it's you against twelve of them.

If your friends act like this, I have two words for you: *distance yourself*. Don't waste time trying to please them and earn their favor. Whatever spin they put on the meaning of "true friendship" is wrong, because girls like this have it backward.

They care more about how *they* feel than how *you* feel.

A true friend doesn't intentionally hurt your feelings. When you're sad, she's sad, and if she needs to apologize, she will. When two girls respect each other this way, valuing what the other one thinks and feels, the best possible friendship results.

If only girls could see what happens at home, in the privacy of their friends' and classmates' bedrooms, I guarantee a lot of cruelty would stop. Consider this behind-the-scenes glimpse of a girl who has been mistreated:

She comes home from school, and immediately her mom asks what's wrong. She can tell something isn't right by her

9

daughter's lifeless face. The daughter says, "Nothing" and goes to her room. The mother debates whether to leave her alone or check in. Fifteen minutes later, she goes to her. She knocks on her daughter's door and asks to come in. The daughter replies, "No," but when the mom hears her sobbing, she enters the bedroom anyway. She finds her daughter curled up in a fetal position on her bed. She is choking back tears, her cheeks are red, and her hair is sticking to her wet face. The mom starts crying too. What happened to her baby?

The mom scoops her daughter into her arms and rocks her. Her strong, big girl is now a limp, vulnerable mess. She hugs her child, kisses her, and tells her she loves her. "Whatever it is," the mom says, "we'll get through it together." The girl is embarrassed to face her mom, so she keeps her head down as she talks. It turns out her old friends ganged up on her today. Again. She tried ignoring them, but they followed her around. They posted a video about her eyebrows on Twitter and called her Thunder Thighs while dressing for PE. They were sneaky, as always, so the teachers didn't see.

With swollen eyes, the girl looks up at her mom and begs to stay home from school. "I can't go back. I can't face them." The mother is sad and furious. She wants to call the principal and the mothers of these girls, but the daughter begs her not to. "You'll make it worse," she says, "Please don't."

I want you to reflect on this scenario a minute, and then ask yourself, "Do I *ever* want to make someone feel that way? Is that the legacy I hope to leave? Do I want girls sobbing uncontrollably as they tell their mothers about me or smiling because I turned their day around? Do my words and behavior *build others up* or *break their spirit?*"

I love girls, and I see so much good in our gender. But lurking inside all of us is a competitive monster that, left unchecked, can create a nightmare. *When girls get jealous or insecure, we start tearing each other down to build ourselves up. We let personal motives take over.* Our competitive monster doesn't go away, and whether we're fifteen years old or fifty, we need to control it.

The easiest way to make yourself look good is to make someone else look bad. It takes no effort, right? So when your insecurities get triggered—maybe because your best friend just announced she's going to Costa Rica for spring break, or your neighbor received a new car for her sixteenth birthday—be aware that your jealous monster will itch to come out. That is the reason you may make flippant comments like, "I heard a family got kidnapped in Costa Rica last year," or "My mother thinks sixteen-year-olds who get new cars are spoiled and entitled."

Love wants what is best for a person, but when you're jealous, you don't desire the best. You may want what is *good,* but the *best?* Well, that means you hope your friend gets a hundred on her history exam when you get an eighty-six. Can you handle that? Will you be okay when she falls in love first . . . wins the election for class president . . . earns a full college scholarship . . . and gets recognized as Most Outstanding Senior?

Time and again, your jealous nature will be tested as good things happen to your friends. Jealousy is natural and nothing to be ashamed of, but you should recognize when your monster gets stirred. Otherwise, it will ruin your relationships.

Love is patient, love is kind, love does not envy or boast (1 Corinthians 13:4). Love is hard to practice in a broken world, but that's no excuse. *Your greatest call in life is to love God. Your second greatest call is to love your neighbor as you love yourself* (Matthew 22:36–40). Are you doing this already, or is there room to improve? Have you figured out yet that when your self-love is pure and genuine, your love for others falls in place?

All this meanness and friends hurting friends has to stop. Maybe if we quit taking our insecurities out on each other, we can love each other properly.

> "THEREFORE ENCOURAGE ONE ANOTHER AND BUILD EACH OTHER UP, JUST AS IN FACT YOU ARE DOING."
> (1 THESSALONIANS 5:11)

Is It True? Is It Good? Is It Useful?

Imagine squeezing an entire tube of toothpaste into the sink. Now imagine putting that glop of toothpaste *back in the tube.*

You can't do it, can you? Once the tooth-paste is out, it's out.

The words you speak are like toothpaste. Once you say them, you can't unsay them. You can't reinsert them in your mouth. Even if you apologize, the mess remains. You've put a stain on someone's heart that is hard to remove.

Before you speak, text, or post on social media, use the Triple Filter Test attributed to Socrates[2]: *Is it true? Is it good? Is it useful?* Imagine how your grandmother might react. Would she be proud of you or mortified? Be smart upfront with what you say or write. Take thirty seconds to think about the weight your words carry before sharing them.

By filtering your words, you avoid messy pile-ups. You help ensure that whatever comes out of your mouth is good and beneficial.

REAL FRIENDS AND 50/50 FRIENDS

When I was your age, I had great friends. But one mistake I sometimes made was expecting my friends to be perfect.

It was an unfair expectation, because only Jesus is the perfect friend. The rest of us are human. We have bad moods; we make mistakes; we say and do things we regret. Leave some allowance for this in your relationships, and understand how *no one friend* can meet all your needs. Everyone has different strengths, and when you love your friends based on their unique strengths, not weaknesses, you'll be happier and more satisfied.

Having a lot of friends takes the pressure off any one person. Your network can look like this:

- Sally, who shares your passion for basketball
- Lizzie, who makes you bust a gut laughing
- Kate, who gives great advice and listens well
- Ann, whose courage inspires you to be brave
- Leah, whose gentle spirit touches your soul and draws you closer to God

Add these friends up, and you get a sum greater than the parts. You can appreciate each girl for who she *is*—not who you *want* her to be. This makes *you* a better friend. It makes you the kind of person others gravitate toward because you're pleasant and not impossible to please.

Just as you shouldn't set the bar too *high* for friends, you also don't want to set it too *low*. In every relationship, you deserve a certain level of trust and respect—and nothing less. Toxic friendships can wreak havoc on your life, your psyche, and your heart, so avoid them. *Don't fall into the trap of putting up with more than you should and paying the price in emotional distress.*

Choosing good friends begins with knowing their heart. Is their heart in the right place? Do they love you even when you're at odds? Are you a better person from knowing them? If you're sick and can't go to school, do they miss you? Do they volunteer to pick up your missed assignments? Is your absence felt when you're not with the group?

Awhile back I heard of a girl who divides her friends into two categories: Real friends and 50/50 friends. Her real friends are the keepers she knows she can count on. Her 50/50 friends are those she's nice to, but she doesn't place her trust in them.

She learned the hard way that all friends aren't equal. Her 50/50 friends were her best friends until they wrote her off one summer and ganged up against her. Although she was heart-broken, this event helped her see the light and find a new tribe. Years later, when the 50/50 friends wanted her back, she stayed with her real friends. While she harbors no hard feelings about what happened, she knows better than to get tangled up in their drama.

Want to know the difference between real friends and 50/50 friends? Here are some hints.

Ten Signs of a 50/50 Friend

1. *She's hot and cold.* She loves you one day, hates you the next. You're never sure where you stand. The inconsistency drives you nuts.
2. *She cuts you down.* This is often done underhandedly. She

may hug you tight while making a jab like, "Your butt
looks big in those jeans—you know I'm joking, right?"

3. *She's available on her terms.* Whether it's a small issue or an
emergency, you can't always rely on her.

4. *She messes with your mind.* She promises to pick you up for a
party—then never shows. She leaves you out on purpose.
She gives you the cold shoulder and makes everything
your fault.

5. *She's competitive.* Your problems secretly delight her; your
success secretly bothers her.

6. *You have fun together, but something about her company brings
you down.* She doesn't really "get" you or appreciate your
true self. She rarely asks about your life because she's too
busy talking about her own.

7. *She constantly switches best friends.* Will it be you, Madison,
or Caroline this week?

8. *Her attitude is "my way or the highway."* One strike and you're
out.

9. *The friendship is one-sided.* You're always the giver, and she's
always the taker.

10. *She's complicated and exhausting.* Does it really have to be
this hard? Must she give you all these headaches?

Ten Signs of a Real Friend

1. *She's loyal and steady.* Even when you argue, you aren't wor-
ried about losing her friendship.

2. *She builds you up.* And should anyone else insult you, she sets the record straight.

3. *She's always there for you.* And if there *is* an emergency, she appears on your doorstep.

4. *She's honest and upfront.* There are no mind games being played.

5. *She's a fan of yours.* When you're playing in a soccer tournament, she screams in the stands and waves the signs she made for you.

6. *You have fun together; after leaving her company, you're uplifted.* You like yourself better when you're with her.

7. *She has other friends and lets you have other friends too.* However, there's a special place in her heart for you that no one can replace, and she lets you know this. She is reassuring.

8. *She respects your perspective and listens when you share it.* She may not always agree with you, but she values your opinions and beliefs.

9. *Your relationship enjoys a healthy balance.* Sometimes you give more, sometimes she gives more, but it all evens out.

10. *What you see is what you get.* She's a breath of fresh air compared to many girls because she doesn't change like a chameleon to blend in with every environment.

You can't force others to be kind, but you can hold yourself to that standard. You can be polite to everyone and ask God to help you see the people who annoy you most (like your pesky brother!) through His loving eyes.

Some mean girls will change. They'll grow up and realize how awful they once were. They may even go back and ask their victims to forgive them. I know this offers little comfort now, but it's good to keep in mind.

Ask God to soften the hearts of mean girls you know, and pray for a breakthrough. It may be five, ten, even twenty years down the road, but girls remember how they acted "back then," and many will regret their behavior. Should they ask you for forgiveness, give it to them. Keep your heart free of grudges and resentment because ultimately, these feelings hurt you more than the events that caused them.

Some mean girls will never change. They'll get married, raise mean daughters and sons, and become one big mean, terrorizing family. It's sad when this cycle repeats itself, but it happens. That is part of the broken world we live in.

All you can control is *you*. By living as God intends, and praying for the grace to be kind, you can enjoy a deep level of happiness, the kind of happiness you've always wanted.

"DEAR FRIENDS, LET US LOVE ONE ANOTHER, FOR LOVE COMES FROM GOD. EVERYONE WHO LOVES HAS BEEN BORN OF GOD AND KNOWS GOD. WHOEVER DOES NOT LOVE DOES NOT KNOW GOD, BECAUSE GOD IS LOVE."
(1 JOHN 4:7–8)

SIMPLE WAYS TO PRACTICE KINDNESS DAILY

- *Call people by name.* Remembering someone's name is a *huge* compliment. It takes two seconds, yet it builds the person up and makes them feel important.

  When I was at cheer camp in eighth grade, a varsity cheerleader I admired, Angela Burton, passed me in the hall and said, "Hey, Kari!" Well, I thought I was big-time because *Angela Burton* knew my name! When Angela and I later became friends, we laughed about this, but it goes to show what a little extra attention can mean.

- *Look out for those who are left out.* That girl who always sits alone at lunch—have you ever wondered what she feels like inside? Don't you think it would make her day if you invited her to sit with you and your friends?

  Then there's that girl who made a terrible mistake by texting a boy inappropriate photos. The whole school is talking about her and avoiding contact. Why not be the one who sits beside her in class or talks to her during break? Your encouraging words may be the only thing that helps her through the day.

  How you treat people in the margins—those excluded, ridiculed, shunned, and teased—speaks volumes. A true Christian doesn't delight in anyone's pain or gang up on them. You aren't called to be best friends with everyone, but you are called to be kind. That is how you become Christlike.

- *Give people the benefit of the doubt.* When you see Instagram photos of friends eating pizza without you, do you assume they left you out on purpose? Are you *certain* they're plotting against you? If so, chill. We can all be a little suspicious and skeptical sometimes, but when you jump to quick conclusions, you tend to assume the worst.

  Do you really want to be the girl who yells at a friend because you weren't invited to her Valentine's party—only to find the Evite two days later, lost in your spam folder? I don't think so. Making rash accusations never ends well. It isn't good for a friendship either.

  Let small injustices roll off your shoulders. Assume the best until someone gives you a reason not to. Most of all, show grace. As you forgive others, God forgives you (Matthew 6:14).

- *Tame your tongue.* Nothing can get you in trouble as fast as your mouth. Before you speak, remember the Triple Filter Test of Socrates (*Is it true? Is it good? Is it useful?*) and add a fourth question: *Is it NECESSARY?* While it may be *true* that Janie said Francis bombed in the talent show, is it really *necessary* to tell Francis? Can any good come from it? While some hard truths should be shared, like telling your friend that her boyfriend is cheating, other truths should be left unsaid. If we all paid attention to the words we blurt out, we could avoid a lot of hurt feelings (Psalm 19:14).

- *Quit judging.* Your friend's family is blowing money, and it bothers you. They spend excessively on houses, horses, and designer clothes. *Have they no shame?* you wonder. *How can they live this way when there are starving kids in Africa?*

While it's normal to have judgmental thoughts, it's wrong to dwell on them. We are called to love, not judge, and it's hard to love someone when you're bashing them in your head. Instead of seeing the negative, focus on the positive. Remember how that same mom who overspends took your mother to chemotherapy last week. Remember how the dad who is a workaholic walked three miles in a snow storm to pick up your baby sister from school.

Leave the judgment to God, and make it your goal to love.

- *Build bridges, not walls.* Did God give you a voice to criticize your friend or lift her up? Do you have eyes to judge appearances or see who may be sad? Are your arms meant to push people away or offer a warm embrace?

God created you to be COMPASSIONATE, not COMPETITIVE. He wants you to make friends, not enemies. The only real enemy in this world is Satan, who seeks to corrupt God's creation. The rest of us are God's children, designed to help each other get to heaven.

Treat others as allies, not enemies, and build bridges that lead to meaningful connections, strong friendships, and abundant joy.

> "THE KING WILL REPLY, 'TRULY I TELL YOU,
> WHATEVER YOU DID FOR ONE OF THE LEAST OF
> THESE BROTHERS AND SISTERS OF MINE, YOU
> DID FOR ME.'"
>
> (MATTHEW 25:40)

THE KINDNESS CHALLENGE (EPHESIANS 4:32)

Every morning when you wake up, you have a choice.

You can use your day to spread kindness or chase popularity. You can either ask, "How can others help me?" or "How can I help others?"

Because here is the deal: *You can't choose both. It really is one or the other.* If your motive is popularity, you'll only have eyes for the cool crowd. Only their circle will do. If you're rejected, it will devastate you because there is no Plan B.

But if your motive is kindness, your options open up. You have eyes for everyone and will go wherever you're needed. Some people think you can't get ahead by being kind, that the only way to achieve your dreams is to connect with movers and shakers, but that's wrong. When you are kind, people try extra-hard to help you. They *want* you to succeed, and somehow, they'll lead you to the connections and opportunities you need.

In the end, love reigns. The most popular girls now may be *mean* and brave, but ultimately, it's the *kind* and brave girls who rise to the top and make a real difference in this world.

Make it your goal to love everyone, then surround yourself with those who do the same.

DISCUSSION QUESTIONS

1. On a scale of one to ten, how important is popularity to you? Have you ever done or said something mean so the popular crowd would like you? If so, how did you feel afterward?

2. Are mean girls loyal? If something bad or embarrassing happened to you, would a mean girl stand by you?

3. How do you treat people who are different: the students with special needs, the social outcasts, the misfits? Do you speak to them or ignore them? Do you laugh when others tell jokes about them?

4. Do you lift your friends up or tear them apart? Have you ever hurt a friend's feelings out of jealousy or anger? If so, how can you control your emotions so it doesn't happen again?

5. Why isn't kindness more common in schools today? What are three easy ways you can practice kindness?

Chapter 2

Confidence

Truth #9: You were born to fly.

hen I was a growing up, I often made simple-minded comments that made people laugh. I'd speak before thinking, demonstrating what I didn't know, and then get teased.

Fortunately, I was a good student. If I hadn't made good grades, I probably would have been labeled *dumb*. Instead I was called "book smart," "naïve," "green," and occasionally "a breath of fresh air." It was often my friends who said these things, and they never meant any harm. Their comments came with a grin or a follow-up like, "That's why I love you."

I learned to laugh at myself and take it in fun. *But deep down, I wished to be different.* I didn't want to be book smart; I wanted to be street smart. I didn't want to be naïve; I wanted to be savvy and sophisticated. I didn't want to be gullible; I wanted to be shrewd.

Because I was young, I kept thinking I'd change. I thought I'd outgrow my innocent outlook on life and morph into a worldly, skeptical adult. I'd lose the rose-colored glasses, grow less optimistic, and stop thinking *like a child.*

But guess what? I didn't change much. Yes, I got wiser. I learned to filter my thoughts before blurting them out. I began to see harsh realities that never registered with me before. But overall, my outlook on life has remained child-like. I still find wonder in ordinary things. I still notice the positive before the negative. I still have an easy time seeing the best in people. I still love to laugh, be silly, and watch Disney movies.

When I *was* a child, I hated the child in me. I felt like she held me back and prevented me from growing up as fast as my peers. But as an adult, I love that child. I see her as a gift from God and the reason I can write messages of hope and encouragement. Now when someone calls me a "breath of fresh air," I take it as a compliment because I realize how important optimism is to a broken, complicated world.

The moral of the story is this: *every characteristic you possess serves a purpose.* They are all tools in the toolbox you'll carry through life. Each tool is necessary and important.

A tool that seems like a curse now, a heavy burden to lug

around, can become a huge blessing when it comes time to use it. Until then, you have to trust the tools God gave you. At some point in your journey, you'll need each one.

Will you ever be perfectly content with your toolbox? Will you ever stop wishing you could trade some of your tools for someone else's? No. You will, however, reach a point where you grow tired of fighting what you can't change about yourself. You'll make a choice to either (1) be miserable about it or (2) accept what you've been given and make the best of it.

I hope you choose the latter. Giving in isn't giving up because leaning into your true nature makes life easier and better. As doors begin to open, you will see how your surrender was actually a victory. *The fears holding you back were unjustified.*

God has great things in store, but to learn what awaits you, you must first be honest with yourself.

"AND WE KNOW THAT IN ALL THINGS GOD WORKS FOR THE GOOD OF THOSE WHO LOVE HIM, WHO HAVE BEEN CALLED ACCORDING TO HIS PURPOSE."

(ROMANS 8:28)

WHAT MAKES YOU DIFFERENT IS
WHAT MAKES YOU GREAT

I live near a junior high school, and I spend a lot of time at my children's elementary school. One thing I've come to notice over the years is how different the students are in these two venues.

At the elementary school, I see lots of personality. The kids are authentic, outgoing, and confident. They run up to hug me and ask random questions, whatever's on their mind. Fashion choices are all over the map. While some kids wear T-shirts and shorts every day (even in thirty-degree weather), others dress as fashionistas.

Anything goes at the elementary school because the overall atmosphere is acceptance. Being different isn't taboo because everyone is different. Nobody knows yet how to be anyone but themselves.

But at the junior high school, the scene is different. I drive by every day and see faces more serious and tentative than the joyful faces at the elementary school. The girls all dress the same—dark jeans, Frye boots, billowy tops, scarves—and to be honest, they look a little scared. I watch them and wonder what happened to the confidence they once had in spades. I ask myself questions like these:

- "What happened to the personalities I once spotted a mile away?"

- "Why do they walk shoulder to shoulder, huddled tight as if they fear a possible attack?"
- "Why is no one smiling?"
- "Why does no one want to be singled out?"

I know junior high is an awkward time. I understand that once self-consciousness and self-awareness kick in, anything that makes you different can add to your insecurity. Still, there's something about this transition that makes me sad. There's something that makes me want to pull the junior high girls aside and reassure them it's okay to be themselves. They don't have to blend in or retreat into their safe shell.

While some girls will rise to the challenge, coming back out of their shell eventually to show their true colors and take on this critical world, others won't. They may spend the rest their lives bottling up their best assets because they believe it's too risky to put themselves out there.

What you should know is this: *You were born to fly. You were made to be authentic, just like the children I see at the elementary school.* What makes you *different* is what makes you *great.* It is a huge part of God's plan for you.

You may be content flying under the radar. Blending in is safe and won't draw negative attention. *But when your goal is to fly under the radar, you're bound to conform.* You'll follow the crowd to avoid the attention that being different brings.

Believe it or not, feeling different is one of the most normal feelings in the world. And if your differences ever make you feel lonely, that's normal too. We all feel different because we *are* different. Remember, never before has there been another human like you *or* me. That is why we have moments where we feel like misfits. That is why we question our design.

God entrusted you with gifts *only you can share.* To tap into your gifts, you must listen to the Holy Spirit, God's presence inside you. This inner voice is your instruction manual that helps you soar. Its purpose is to lift your feet off the ground.

You face overwhelming pressure to conform. At your age, it is all about acting alike, talking alike, and falling in line like a row of ducks. But when you make yourself a carbon copy of your friends, you become replaceable. You make yourself interchangeable for thirty other girls.

Really now, what's the point of that?

Think about your favorite people on the planet. Why do you love them? What attracts you to their company? Chances are, it's because they are unique. You've never met anyone like them—nor will you. What makes them remarkable is their willingness to shine as an original. You couldn't clone them if you tried.

This may sound strange, but feeling different is a *gift.* It reveals what is special about you. It reminds you that the world's way isn't God's way. It makes you pause before conforming. To pioneer your own path, you have to *tune into* your uncomfortable feelings and listen to what they tell you. Even pain serves a purpose. It is there to guide you, not hold you back.

You'll always be tempted to hide what makes you different. You'll always be tempted to settle for normal, which isn't striving for much. But when you bury your unique qualities, you bury your potential, because *it's through your uniqueness that your best opportunities emerge.*

Whatever you'd like to cover up, I guarantee it is the *exact* thing God has given you to help build His kingdom.

Aim *higher* than normal. Rise above the crowd without fear, shame, or apology. Birds fly in a flock, but an eagle soars alone. Do you want to be an eagle? Do you long to satisfy that urge that wishes to see more, be more, and do more (Isaiah 40:31)?

You have the gifts and capacity. You have wings to fly. And once you know your talents, you can take any vision God's placed on your heart and rise to achieve it.

> "FOR THIS REASON I REMIND YOU TO FAN INTO FLAME THE GIFT OF GOD, WHICH IS IN YOU THROUGH THE LAYING ON OF MY HANDS. FOR THE SPIRIT GOD GAVE US DOES NOT MAKE US TIMID, BUT GIVES US POWER, LOVE AND SELF-DISCIPLINE."
>
> (2 TIMOTHY 1:6–7)

Is There Hope for Quiet Girls?

When I was young, I was very shy. I liked to observe life instead of jumping into the action. While neighborhood kids played games in our front yard, I stayed in my bedroom reading. Even though I could hear everyone having fun, I was perfectly content in my private world.

Being an introvert, however, sometimes made it hard for me to connect with others. I longed to be like the outgoing kids who never seemed uncomfortable in social settings. When you're shy or quiet, it's easy to go unnoticed. It's easy to get overshadowed by big person- alities who don't hide in their shell or hesitate to put themselves "out there."

What I learned over time is that there *is* hope for quiet girls. Yes, our world is made for extroverts, but with extra courage, an introvert can adapt. How? By learning to come out of your shell, push past your comfort zone, and pursue passions that bring you alive. *Because when you feel alive, you forget to be shy.* You get so caught up in the moment—and the connections you make—you gain the sense of belonging you crave.

I used to believe my introverted nature was a handicap, but now I consider it an asset. It is introverts, after all, who tend to be deep thinkers, good listeners, and keen observers. We notice when people are hurting. We recognize life nuances that others miss. We are highly in tune with our thoughts, feelings, and emotions, and as a result, we often succeed at art and innovation.

So if you're quiet or shy, have faith in yourself. Don't discount your future or assume you can't chase your dreams as well as a social butterfly can. God gave you talents that can help you build bridges to others. As your talents touch the mind, heart, and soul of others, you learn to embrace yourself.

Think about what brings you alive. Is it the tingle in your fingers when you play piano? The rush in your body when you dance on stage and feel music pulsate under your feet? The intense curiosity sparked when you study biology? Whatever you love most, that is probably your ticket to overcoming shyness. It can help you to live as boldly and bravely as an extrovert.

God created us for community. And when you share your gifts, you draw people in. You form connections based on the real you. You find encouragement to venture further from your shell and put yourself "out there" with confidence.

It's okay to need time alone to recharge. It's okay to enjoy life as an observer at times. The key for quiet girls is to strike a healthy balance. Use your shell when necessary, but don't get too cozy. The world needs your talents, and no matter how introverted you are, God will provide ways to pass on the gifts He gave you.

"IN THE SAME WAY, FAITH BY ITSELF, IF IT IS NOT ACCOMPANIED BY ACTION, IS DEAD."

(JAMES 2:17)

STEP ONE: RECOGNIZING YOUR GIFTS

A lot of people believe they don't have talent. They see talent in others, but not themselves. I don't buy that for one second. If you're a child of God, which we all are, you have talent. You have gifts your Maker instilled in you to help you glorify Him.

While you and I may have different gifts, it's the same Spirit that distributes them. While we may serve in different ways, it's the same God at work inside us (1 Corinthians 12:4–6).

For some people, talent is readily apparent. We've all met or heard of prodigies whose abilities are off the charts. They're the Taylor Swifts of the world, the lightning in a bottle. From the moment they first strum a guitar, pick up a football, or sketch a drawing, the signs of greatness are there. It's clear to see how promising their future is because of where they start.

Then there are the rest of us, the non-prodigies who have hobbies and interests, but no readily apparent, supernatural gifts. We know what we *like* to do, but we're not sure what we're *meant* to do. Or maybe we know what we're meant to do, but we face obstacles like having more passion than talent or not having the resources to start.

Either way, we must work harder than the prodigies. They have a head start, and while we can catch up on some level, we'll probably never be in the same league if they match our efforts.

And frankly, that is okay. There's room in the sky for eagles to soar at every level. Some will fly at higher altitudes than you, and some will fly lower. Some will have bigger fan clubs, fancier tricks, and better speed. You can spend your time being jealous of other eagles and keeping a constant eye on them, or you can pour your energy into making yourself a better eagle.

The choice is yours.

So let's start with the basics: Do you know your talents? Have you assessed your strengths and weaknesses? If not, consider these questions:

- What do I do better than my friends? What are my strong subjects in school? Does my family rely on me for certain jobs? What activities come naturally for me?
- What do I see better than most people? What's obvious to me that isn't obvious to others? Can I read emotions? Do I have a knack for design? Can I watch a dance routine and pick it up? Can I make art out of junk?
- What puts me in a "zone"? Would I rather craft with my hands or my mind? Do I have more imagination or logic?
- What do people compliment me on? Do I hear feedback on my photography? My articles in the school paper? The parties I plan? My teaching skills?
- What gets me so engrossed I lose track of time? What could I do all day long and never get bored?
- What would I do if failure or rejection didn't scare me? What's my dream job?
- What is my happy place? Where do I come alive? Am I happiest when I'm singing? Playing tennis? Performing

in community theater? Walking in the woods? Playing with my puppy?

- On a scale of one to ten, how do I rank in these categories?

  _ Emotional intelligence (ability to understand what I'm feeling)
  _ Social intelligence (ability to read others and pick up on social cues)
  _ Academic intelligence (school performance when I apply myself)
  _ Body intelligence (motor skills and abilities)
  _ Spiritual intelligence (understanding of God and eternity)

The word *smart* is a broad umbrella. There are many ways to be intelligent because talent takes on many forms. While school is very important and crucial to a healthy adult life, not all talents can be measured in a classroom. So if you're giving your best and struggling in certain subjects, don't sell yourself short. Don't assume you must be "dumb" because you can't cut it somewhere. You can and you will—just maybe not in calculus.

Depending on what you show a knack for, your intelligence could fall in one of these areas:

- People smart
- Numbers smart

- Heart smart
- Food smart
- Fashion smart
- Sports smart
- Body smart
- Music smart
- Animal smart
- Word smart
- Art smart

The list goes on.

When you use your talents, God gives you more. When you don't use them, you lose them. It's a waste to let your talents go unused. It also makes it hard for you to be happy when others apply their talents and succeed. When you aren't living up to your potential, you'll envy anyone who does.

Identifying your talents is the first step. The second step is developing them. To go from "good" to "great" takes dedication and persistence.

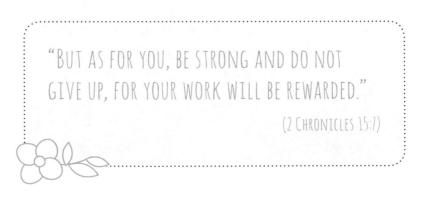

"BUT AS FOR YOU, BE STRONG AND DO NOT GIVE UP, FOR YOUR WORK WILL BE REWARDED."

(2 CHRONICLES 15:7)

STEP TWO: HONING YOUR GIFTS

Picasso didn't become Picasso in a week. Bill Gates didn't build Microsoft in a year. Even if you're a prodigy, you must still work hard. You have to stay committed when most people would give up.

Focus on what you can do *today.* Practice what you love for an hour—playing guitar, writing poetry, testing recipes—and repeat the process tomorrow. After a few weeks, your practice will form a habit. You'll see progress that encourages you to press on.

There are no shortcuts to becoming an eagle, although we all look for them. Developing your talents may mean giving up what you want now—i.e., watching TV or going to a party—for what you want later. But if you enjoy the process, it won't feel like a sacrifice. You can celebrate how far you've come instead of lamenting how far you have to go.

All too often, people give up too soon. They set their expectations too high and quit the second they fail. Show yourself grace by allowing room to make mistakes. You may fall before you fly, but if you see failure as *part* of your story—not the *end* of your story—it won't keep you down for long.

Consider this example of how practice pays off: Years ago, I had a line of poem prints I sold at arts and crafts shows. At one show, there was an artist generating buzz. Her stationary was amazing, very whimsical and eye-catching, and from morning until night her booth remained packed.

By all accounts, this girl had "made it." She had a large staff, and they'd just been to an Atlanta Gift Mart to take her work national. This hometown hero was about to explode, and being in on the secret was pretty cool.

When I returned home, I raved about this artist to a customer who owned a stationary store. "You *have* to carry her work," I insisted. "They're the cutest cards ever!"

A funny look came over this store owner's face. After thinking a moment, she slipped into her storage room. A minute later she came back holding a pack of note cards. They were white and totally blah. The line art looked like a child's drawing—and not a talented child either.

"We carried that artist's cards a few years ago," the store owner said, "and they didn't sell."

I couldn't believe this was the same artist. To say she had improved was an understatement. Her cards at the craft show I'd just been to were authentic and bold, but these were, well, not. My guess was that it took trial and error to develop a signature style. She had to make mistakes to later accomplish a look that would hit.

The expert at *anything* was once a beginner. Like you, they doubted themselves and wondered what business they had pretending to have talent. What if that artist had quit? What if she never made it to craft shows and the Atlanta Gift Mart because her early products didn't sell?

Seeing how she reinvented herself was a powerful lesson for me. I hope it sticks with you too.

You'll never be as talented as you wish you were. You'll never be completely confident in your work. And while you don't want to share your work too soon, because it's better to wow people than underwhelm them, you also don't want to be so scared and self-critical you never take a chance, never step out, never show the world what you've got.

Remember, you were born to fly. And when you clamp your wings down, you miss out on God's plan for you.

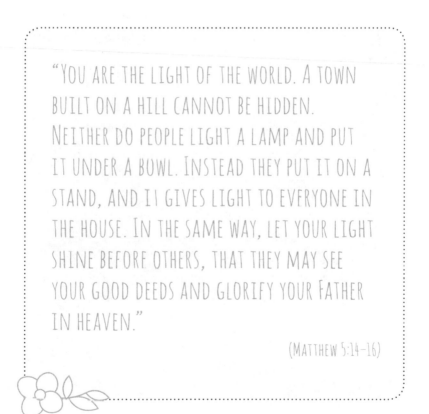

"YOU ARE THE LIGHT OF THE WORLD. A TOWN BUILT ON A HILL CANNOT BE HIDDEN. NEITHER DO PEOPLE LIGHT A LAMP AND PUT IT UNDER A BOWL. INSTEAD THEY PUT IT ON A STAND, AND IT GIVES LIGHT TO EVERYONE IN THE HOUSE. IN THE SAME WAY, LET YOUR LIGHT SHINE BEFORE OTHERS, THAT THEY MAY SEE YOUR GOOD DEEDS AND GLORIFY YOUR FATHER IN HEAVEN."

(MATTHEW 5:14–16)

STEP THREE: TAKING OFF

The point of flying like an eagle isn't to show off. It is to point others to God.

So if you're reluctant about being on display, take yourself out of the equation. Forget about *your* fears, *your* worries, *your* doubts. Stop thinking about possible judgment and criticism. Focus instead on God and find purpose in serving Him. Whatever talents you share, share them with all your heart.

What makes you *different* is what makes you *great*. So when you question your design, when you wish to change what can't be changed, remember God has a plan. He made you to serve your generation. Every detail about you is part of His amazing vision.

You're an original, so act like one. Chart your own course and hold your head high, knowing that anything you do, you're doing for Him.

DISCUSSION QUESTIONS

1. Do you ever miss the little, naïve girl you used to be, the one who didn't care so much about what other people thought? How can you reconnect with her?

2. What is one trait you wish you could change about yourself? Can you think of how God might use that trait for good down the road?

3. Has anyone ever shot down your dreams? If so, did it motivate you more or make you want to quit?

4. Why does bottling up your personality create tension? Is it possible to discover God's unique plan for you when your life is a replica of someone else's life?

5. If our God is a God of miracles, what miracles might He work through you?

Chapter 3

Reputation

Truth #8: Today's choices set the stage for your reputation.

When you were born, your parents or guardians received the privilege of naming you.

Chances are, they spent the first few weeks of your life staring into your small eyes and repeating your name again and again to make it stick. They may have wondered, "Did I choose the right name? Does my baby *look* like a Margaret? Will her name match her personality as she grows up?"

With some time, your name kicked in. It started to roll off people's tongues with no hesitation. Today, you *own* your name. It is so intertwined with your identity that it's hard to imagine a time when anyone doubted the fit.

Whether you realize it or not, your name is important. As something you carry through life, it's worth taking seriously. Every choice you make affects how your name resonates in people's minds. Over time, your peers form a collective opinion about your name based on your choices. This gives birth to your *reputation*.

What do people automatically think when your name comes up? What pops in their head in the first five seconds? Is it "Oh, she's so sweet" or "Did you hear what she did under the bleachers at the football game last week?"

If it is the latter, you have a problem. Your reputation is only as good as your worst choice, and left unchecked, poor choices can create damage that's hard to recover from.

You and your name will be joined at the hip forever. By making a conscientious choice to protect it, you can honor your name and save yourself a lot of grief.

"A GOOD NAME IS MORE DESIRABLE THAN GREAT RICHES; TO BE ESTEEMED IS BETTER THAN SILVER OR GOLD."

(PROVERBS 22:1)

A GOOD REPUTATION = A SERIES OF GOOD CHOICES

If a girl makes an A on an English paper, does that make her a star student?

If a boy hits a home run, does that make him a stellar athlete?

Anybody can be successful every *once* in a while. But what people who achieve greatness have in common is consistency. A star student makes lots of As, not one. A stellar athlete makes multiple home runs, not one fluke hit.

The same is true for your reputation. It isn't enough to make one good choice and go back to following the wrong crowd. The choices you make reveal your character. They reflect the moral fiber—or lack of it—that exists inside you.

A great reputation is built through commitment and self-discipline. It emerges when you stay on track and choose well consistently. You know how a snowball starts small, but then gains size and momentum as it rolls down a hill? That is how your reputation works. Over time, your little choices accumulate. They keep growing and piling on top of each other until one day, you realize how *real* your reputation is.

Then the question becomes: Are you proud of your reputation—or ashamed to claim it?

What you should know is this: *Today's choices set the stage for your reputation. Nobody becomes a "bad girl" overnight.* It all starts with the baby steps and choices you make now. So when you experiment with that first beer . . . that first cigarette . . . that first boy, you open a gate that's hard to close. You start down a one-way street with no easy U-turn in sight.

Experimentation can snowball over time and land you in the wrong crowd. This crowd may be ridiculously fun, but they aren't friends with your best interests in mind.

And while it's never too late to turn your life around, you can't make people forget your mistakes. Whatever choices you make, get ready to live with them. Sadly, one dumb decision can follow you the rest of your life.

Am I saying you have to be perfect? That after one slip, all hope is lost? No. Nobody makes good choices all the time. We're all human, and yes, we all make mistakes.

But when you stumble—or fall flat on your face—take your sin straight to God. Pray for help to do better, because only by God's grace can any of us stay on track (or get back on it). The evil forces in your life are led by Satan's attempt to separate you from God. Satan is powerful, but he is *no match* for God. Through Christ you can gain the strength to resist any temptation that seeks to interrupt God's plan for you (Philippians 4:13).

What if you already have a bad reputation? What if you've made so many poor choices in the past that your peers can't see you in a favorable light? If this is your story, keep the faith. Don't resign yourself to being a "bad girl" or assume there is no way out. Through God all things are possible (Matthew 19:26), and by living your life aligned with Christ, you become a new creation (2 Corinthians 5:17).

Will restoring your name be easy? No. Will it take time? Yes. Will some people hold past choices over your head even after you change? Probably. But that doesn't matter because ultimately, God's opinion of your reputation is the only one that counts.

So channel your efforts into pleasing Him. Let God redeem your mistakes and give you the peace that transcends all understanding (Philippians 4:7). God will bless you with friends who see your future, not your past, and in the process you'll gain a greater appreciation for God's mercy and unconditional love.

Whether your reputation is shiny and bright or dull and tarnished, you need God. It doesn't matter how faithful you've been in the past, because good people fall into corruption *all the time*. The moment you think you're safe against stumbles, completely immune to the risks everyone else faces, is the moment your risk increases.

"DO NOT BE DECEIVED: 'BAD COMPANY RUINS GOOD MORALS.'"

(1 CORINTHIANS 15:33 ESV)

Quick Quiz: Do You Notice Red Flags?

A guy you like has invited you to a concert. You want to go, but since the concert is out of town, you're scared your dad will say no.

He advises you to tell your dad you're spending the night at a friend's house because sometimes, it's easier to ask for forgiveness than permission. He also asks that you keep this date a secret because his ex-girlfriend thinks they're still exclusive. She'll go haywire if she finds out about you.

What are your thoughts of this guy?

A. He is fun, cool, and adventurous. His spontaneity will keep things exciting.

B. You can't believe he chose *you* over his gorgeous ex! You don't know what he sees in you, but it feels good.

C. You don't trust him. Despite his winning smile, he isn't a nice guy.

D. Forget this! Dump this creep already so you can hang out with your friends.

If you answered "C" or "D," your instincts are spot-on. A liar is a liar, and a guy who can't respect your dad enough to tell him the truth won't respect you either.

Asking you to keep the date a secret is another red flag. A healthy relationship stays in the light; there's no sneaking around or making up stories. Since you know that he lies, he's probably still dating his girlfriend and wants a fling with you. If that doesn't bother you, keep this in mind: if he'll do it *for* you, he'll do it *to* you.

Relationships with cheaters never go well. Cut your losses early by not getting involved.

THE TROUBLE WITH TROUBLE IS IT ALWAYS STARTS OFF FUN

You've probably been told to steer clear of bad influences.

But has anyone ever mentioned how charming and fun the bad influences can be?

In most cases, they are funny. Quick-witted. Physically attractive and socially adept. They have inside jokes and exciting lives. Being in their circle is like being in an exclusive club. Only the elite receive an invitation.

And here's a caveat: bad influences aren't entirely bad. They have good and redeeming qualities too—qualities that can help you justify your relationship with them even when you know it's not right.

When you spend time with a certain group, you gravitate to their way of thinking. You warm up to their ideas and grow desensitized to what may have shocked you initially. Once your sense of normal gets altered, the old values you once held true fly out the window. Your morals get compromised.

If you believe you can hang with a wilder crowd and not have their influence rub off, you're fooling yourself. The company you keep has a *huge* bearing on your choices. You won't lift the wild crowd up to higher standards; they'll drag you down to theirs. As the saying in addiction recovery programs goes, "If you hang around the barbershop long enough, you're going to get a haircut."

For better or for worse, *your friends matter.* Besides your family, they're the biggest influence on your life. All it takes is one person, one seemingly harmless friend or boyfriend, to lead you astray.

The best time to get out of an unhealthy relationship is early, before you're deeply invested. *Pay attention to red flags like bad vibes and feelings of unease, because that's God speaking to you.* God will provide warning signs that a relationship isn't right, but He won't chase you down. It's your choice whether you tune into His clues or ignore them.

Does your peer group lead you off track? Consider these questions:

- Where do your happy moments come from? Are they rooted in good choices or bad choices? If you're happy because the coolest cheerleaders brag on you for getting wasted at last night's party, something is wrong. Straighten up your act and pick new friends.
- How do you feel *the morning after* a night when you made questionable choices, when you're alone in your bedroom? Do you feel good about what you did with your girlfriends or boyfriend, or do you feel guilty/ashamed/lonely? The truth that speaks the morning after, when your mind is still and quiet, is crucial to your Christian journey.
- Do your friends applaud you for doing what you know is wrong (i.e., stealing mascara from the drugstore or cheating on final exams)? Is their idea of right and wrong different from what your parents and church leaders say? Any "friend" who likes you best when you compromise your morals, act out, or rebel isn't a friend at all.
- Do your friends care about your hopes and dreams? Do they have hopes and dreams too? Friends who lack ambition make it hard for you to reach your goals. If you have to stay home to finish a project, do your friends understand, or do they get mad that you're bailing on them?
- Do you and your friends have deep conversations?

Do you connect on a spiritual level? Do your friends trigger feelings of peace and self-acceptance inside you, or are your relationships superficial? If you find yourself losing sight of God, downplaying your faith, or ignoring your faith altogether, you're with the wrong crowd.

- Are your friends obsessed with parties? Does life revolve around having a good time? Are you stuck in a cycle of doing the same thing every weekend, with no real growth? Good friends help you become a better person. They inspire you to aim higher and stretch yourself in a positive direction.

Let's be clear: your choices are your choices. And hanging around a bad influence is a choice. So while you're more likely to make poor decisions when you're in the wrong crowd, you can't blame them for your choices. *You* reserve the right to say no. *You're* the one responsible for protecting your name and reputation.

Your choices today affect your opportunities tomorrow. With every vice comes a trade-off, and as my friend's mother used to tell her, "A moment of pleasure, a lifetime of regret." Even a brief period of living on the edge can set up roadblocks for you later.

Consider this example: When I was in college, I knew a number of people who went crazy their first semester. They played hard and were the life of every party. But come December, when grades came out, they paid the price. Their grade point average (GPA) was so low they spent the rest of their college years struggling to raise it to a C or B, because an A average was already out of the question.

That wild and crazy stage cost some people their dreams. One guy who wanted to go to medical school studied intensely from then on and never could pull up his GPA enough to qualify. Does that sound worth it to you, no medical school in exchange for one semester of parties and fun?

It's hard to think about these things when you're caught up in the moment, but you should. After college graduation, you'll face a highly competitive workplace. You'll be up against job candidates more qualified than you. To get a job that pays well, you need every advantage you can get. You can't afford to shoot yourself in the foot by creating predicaments you could have avoided.

Imagine where you'd like to be in five, ten, and fifteen years. Write down your aspirations on paper, and then work backward to ask yourself how today's choices may impact you getting there.

Do you hope to get into law school? Remember that when a friend encourages you to try drugs. The state-regulated boards that have to certify and accept you will ask you questions about drug and alcohol use and convictions, DUIs, and other offenses. Imagine trying to explain why you thought it was okay to experiment with marijuana or drink and drive. Imagine having your future in the hands of a third party that decides you aren't trustworthy to help and protect others because of bad decisions you made earlier.

You'd be embarrassed and heartbroken, wouldn't you? You might wish someone had told you earlier how the past can haunt you.

Let's bring it closer to home now. Do you hope to get in a sorority? Remember that when boys push you to have sex. I've seen many beautiful, popular girls get dropped from every sorority because of their promiscuity and reputation. What happens behind closed doors does *not* remain secret. Sooner or later, the word gets out.

And then there are the more serious consequences of having sex, like getting pregnant or acquiring a sexually trans-mitted disease (STD). Even with your *first* sexual encounter, you run the risk of these events. Despite claims by our culture, premarital sex isn't cool and glamorous. It creates very real bur-dens like emotional pain and physical risks that can rob you of your dreams overnight.

All your choices matter, but the choices you make on Friday and Saturday night can make or break you. They follow you through junior high, high school, college, and beyond. Yes, God is merciful, but people aren't always as forgiving. They won't wipe your slate clean and forget it all.

Ask God to help you choose well, then pray for friends who do the same.

> "FINALLY, BROTHERS AND SISTERS, WHATEVER
> IS TRUE, WHATEVER IS NOBLE, WHATEVER
> IS RIGHT, WHATEVER IS PURE, WHATEVER IS
> LOVELY, WHATEVER IS ADMIRABLE—IF ANY-
> THING IS EXCELLENT OR PRAISEWORTHY, THINK
> ABOUT SUCH THINGS."
>
> (PHILIPPIANS 4:8)

MAKING A HABIT OF GOOD CHOICES

Do you dream of the day you'll have freedom? Are you eager for a life with no rules, no restrictions, and no nagging adults?

When you leave home, you'll get the freedom you crave. You'll enter a world where you can do what you want, when you want, with whomever you please. You can eat pizza for breakfast and cake for lunch. You can watch TV all day and skip class. You can take the money your parents deposited in your checking account for tuition and blow it on a new wardrobe.

There's only one catch: your choices will have consequences. Whatever you choose, you have to live with the outcome.

Eat poorly and your body pays the price. Skip class and your grades suffer. Squander your parent's money and you lose trust, credibility, and spending privileges.

Making good choices is a habit. It requires self-control, discipline, and thinking twice. By practicing on small choices, you lay the groundwork for bigger choices to come. You also prove you're mature enough to take on more responsibility.

As Luke 16:10 says, "Whoever can be trusted with very little can also be trusted with much, and whoever is dishonest with very little will also be dishonest with much."

You can't make negative choices and expect a positive life. You can't expect adults or peers to take you seriously if you're always impulsive or prone to taking the path of least resistance.

This is *your life*. Don't waste it by putting your future on the line for fleeting thrills. Don't let other persuade you against your will. *Your chief asset right now is your name.* You don't own a house. You don't have cars and worldly possessions. If you needed a job to earn money, your name is your selling point. So when people hear it, do they make positive or negative associations? Does your name add value to your life—or is it destroying your opportunities?

Clearly God can restore anything. No mistake is too big for Him to forgive and forget. But restoring your name among people is another story, especially those with set opinions that don't easily change. And while you can't dwell on their opinions or spend your life chasing their approval, you also can't ignore how the talk of your reputation may impede your life. Since it's easier to keep a good name than it is to rebuild a bad one, think twice before doing anything that puts your name at risk.

God designed you to make positive choices. By making a habit of good choices now, you'll live better, sleep better, and be in a better position to continue choosing well when the stakes of your decisions are high.

DISCUSSION QUESTIONS

1. What three words would your peers use to describe you?

2. Have you made choices that might contribute to a bad reputation? If so, how can you choose better next time?

3. Where do you see yourself in ten years? Do your current choices support your dreams, or could they hinder them?

4. On a scale of one to ten, where is your self-control? Will you be able to monitor yourself in college without an adult keeping tabs? How can you keep yourself accountable?

5. Is there a negative influence nudging (or pulling) you down the wrong path? If so, how can you resist that pressure? What positive influences in your life keep you grounded?

Chapter 4

Interacting with Boys

I n my community, there is a woman named Donna Greene.[3] Donna knows girls. Donna loves girls. Donna has spent the past forty years ministering to teenage girls, helping them find Christ and cope with the struggles of growing up by applying truth.

More than four thousand girls have participated in Donna's Community Ministry for Girls. She's amazing, and what I love most about Donna is how she invests in these girls' lives. Long after high school graduation she stays involved, attending their weddings, meeting their newborn babies in the hospital, and showing up for special moments.

At the wedding reception of one couple in their late twenties, something interesting happened to Donna. She was making her rounds in the ballroom when suddenly she looked up and realized a circle of young men had surrounded her. The huddle formed quickly, creating a seal so tight she couldn't escape if she wanted to.

One guy, the spokesman, introduced himself and said, "We just wanted you to know that when we were in high school, we had an I-Hate-Donna-Greene Club."

Donna looked at the young man perplexed. What on earth was he saying?

"We'd get together and talk about you," the young man continued, "because *all those girls of yours* wouldn't do anything with us."

He didn't qualify his statements, which left Donna more perplexed. She had no idea where this conversation was headed or how was she supposed to reply. But as it turned out, a reply wasn't necessary. What played out next spoke for itself.

In unison, in a gesture they had clearly planned, these young men held out their hands to Donna and asked to shake her hand.

"Thank you, Donna," the leader explained, "because these are the girls we're marrying."

———

As I'm sure you know, we live in a world that is fast and sexually charged. You're part of a generation that competes for boys and gives them what they want to win their affection. Waiting for males to act first is old school; if you like what you see, you're told to go for it.

But seeking Mr. Right this way inadvertently makes you Ms. Wrong. *Guys may be dying to date Ms. Wrong, but they won't be dying to marry her.*

This chapter is one of the most important sections of this book. Of all the forces that can lure you off track, nothing works quicker than a misguided quest for love. You'll hear a lot of conflicting advice on finding your heart's desire, and my intention is to set the record straight. I want to help you connect the dots between boys, dating, marriage, and sex.

"FOR IN HIM ALL THINGS WERE CREATED: THINGS IN HEAVEN AND ON EARTH, VISIBLE AND INVISIBLE, WHETHER THRONES OR POWERS OR RULERS OR AUTHORITIES; ALL THINGS HAVE BEEN CREATED THROUGH HIM AND FOR HIM."

(COLOSSIANS 1:16)

Why do the trusted adults in your life promote purity and saving sex for marriage? Why would teenage boys who once had an "I-Hate-Donna-Greene Club" later change their tune and publicly *thank* this mentor of young girls for encouraging them to stay virtuous and resist pressure from boys, friends, and the world at large?

The answers are coming, but upfront you should know that your journey toward womanhood begins with one Man. Only He can affirm your worth. Only He can lead you to love. Only He can help you make choices that protect your heart, your future, and what God has in store for you.

WHO IS THE CENTER OF YOUR UNIVERSE?

Somewhere in science class, you learned about the solar system. You studied the planets, the sun, and how they relate in the universe.

In many ways, your life is like a planet. You were designed to revolve around a sun. Without your sun, you can't exist. You lose your source of light, life, and gravity to stay in orbit.

So let me ask this: Who is the "sun" in your life? Who is the center of your universe? Who nourishes and sustains you, giving purpose to your day and propelling you out of bed each morning?

God designed you to revolve around Christ. Only His Son can function as your sun. You can put other people and passions in Christ's place, but eventually they'll fail you. Sooner or later, your orbit will be rocked.

Keeping Christ at the center of your universe is harder than it sounds. Because you're human and part of a fallen species that is sinful and selfish by nature (due to original sin), you'll constantly fight the urge to make other things your number one. It might be something good—like friends, good grades, a love for soccer—or it might be something self-destructive. Either way, when anything other than Christ becomes your sun, you have a false idol. You've taken an earthly pleasure that can never satisfy your deepest needs and made it the center of your existence.

Why is this relevant to boys? *Because one common mistake girls make is putting boys at the center of their universe.* Besides setting you up for disappointment, this puts unfair pressure on the boys. It forces them into a role they were never meant to play, to be a girl's end-all, be-all, everything.

Girls who obsess over boys and center their lives around them have always been around. However, this phenomenon is amplified today due to (1) a rising culture of female aggressiveness that makes it socially acceptable to chase boys and (2) technology. Thanks to cell phones and social media, you can access boys all the time. You don't have to wait for them to call you; you can call them. You don't have to wonder what they're doing; you can simply text them or check their Twitter feed.

Chasing and obsessing over boys has practically become a national sport for girls. And while some celebrate this as a victory for our gender, I believe it's the downfall of healthy relationships. All this excessive attention and communication actually smothers boys. It makes them want to run the other way and find a girl who isn't overbearing.

What you should know is this: *Chasing boys doesn't make you cool. It makes you a nuisance.* One thing I hear repeatedly from moms with sons is how girls today are very forward. They constantly call and text, and the boys don't like it.

Boys enjoy and need a challenge. They lose interest when a girl takes the lead. You may think you're making progress, but really you're making yourself look bad. You're also damaging your internal spirit, because your self-perception is as important as the public perception you create. God created you to guard your heart (Proverbs 4:23), not freely give it away to the guys who come and go.

When you do reach out to a boy, it isn't just him receiving your message. It's his circle of friends and family, too, because more often than not, he's with other people.

Imagine all his buddies at baseball practice watching his phone rattle on the bench in the dugout. After the third or fourth time, they gather around. They start quizzing him and teasing him. *Dude, who keeps texting you? What does she want? She's hot for you, isn't she? Seriously, does she ever leave you alone?*

Imagine his family at the dinner table, enjoying a meal. They're getting a little irritated as you blow up his phone and interrupt their conversation. "Why does Jennifer call you all the time?" his little sister asks, addressing the elephant in the room. "Are you her only friend?"

Am I telling you it's wrong to speak or interact with boys? Of course not. It's fine to show interest in a boy. It's okay to initiate conversation, smile, make eye contact, and express enough interest to let him know you'd like him to pursue you. If he calls first, call him back. If he texts you, text him back.

But don't be desperate. Because when you ask a boy out, plan dates, and call and text excessively, that's how you come across. You also want to avoid building your life around a boy. Not only does this hurt your relationship, it holds *you* back from achieving your own goals and pursuing your interests.

One regret I often hear from women is the regret of dating too seriously as teenagers. Instead of investing so much time in a serious relationship, they wish they'd invested that time in themselves.

You have gifts to change the world. And when you don't use them, when you hide them or forget they exist, your gifts go to waste. You may think you'll never make a boy your number one, never push Christ aside or give up personal dreams to keep your boyfriend happy, but at some point you'll be tempted. When the right boy comes along, you'll want to drop everything and follow him.

Following your true love may work once you reach marrying age, but doing it now—in your teen years, when your identity is still forming—is a poor use of precious time.

> "FOR IN CHRIST ALL THE FULLNESS OF THE
> DEITY LIVES IN BODILY FORM, AND IN CHRIST
> YOU HAVE BEEN BROUGHT TO FULLNESS. HE IS
> THE HEAD OVER EVERY POWER AND AUTHORITY."
> (COLOSSIANS 2:9–10)

WHOEVER HE IS, HE'S NOT WORTH IT

When I was in the eighth grade, I had my first big crush. We had pre-algebra together, and even though he didn't pay attention to me, I was very self-conscious around him.

I needed glasses to see the chalkboard, but letting my crush see my nerd look was unthinkable. So instead of keeping up in pre-algebra, I fell behind. I made a C and wound up needing a tutor. All because I was embarrassed to wear glasses around "him."

When I think about that year, that crush, and that silly fear of my eyewear, I want to reach back through time and shake my thirteen-year-old self. The fact that a good student would accept a C for a boy who barely acknowledged her existence is compelling proof that (1) I was an idiot and (2) girls will do crazy things for love sometimes.

If you haven't already, you'll meet a boy one day who reduces your IQ. All logic will vanish as you fall under the spell of his crooked smile, dreamy eyes, sense of humor, and funny jokes. When you're in class, you'll daydream about him. When you walk the halls, you'll look for his face in the crowd, hoping for a quick fix to get you through the day.

Welcome to the Land of Romance, my dear. I hope you enjoy the stay.

Falling for a new crush is intense. You may think you'll never fall so hard again. But you will . . . again and again you will. New crushes round the corner all the time, and each one will cast a different spell on you.

Sometimes your crush will crush back. You'll discover your feelings are mutual and fall head-over-heels together. I won't lie; this part is awesome. It's fun and thrilling to realize a boy likes you as much as you like him—maybe more. The bliss of being together makes it hard to be apart. As your romance blooms, the rest of your life may seem small and insignificant in comparison. You may be tempted to postpone your plans so you and your new love can carve out more time together.

But please don't. Don't put off your ambitions. Don't re-arrange your life. Don't over-invest in the relationship. Enjoy dating him, but don't put your boyfriend center stage. No matter how great your relationship is, it *won't last*. You won't marry the boy you date in junior high or high school, and if by some remote chance you do, you're still doing yourself a disservice by focusing too much time on him.

Why? Because now is the time to be chasing dreams, not your future husband. Now is the time to cultivate the God-given talents that will enable you to (1) figure out your life calling and (2) get a job to support yourself.

You may be thinking, *But I just want to be a wife and mom. Why do I need a job if I never plan to work?* Here's the answer: *because every able woman should know how to earn a living.* What if you don't meet the man of your dreams until you're thirty? Who will pay your bills until then? What if you do marry out of college, but ten years later your husband gets sick, and your family needs you to bring home a salary? Will you be capable?

I started dating my husband when I was twenty-three, which is relatively young. Within a month we knew we'd get married, but we waited three years because he lived in a different city and I loved my job. To this day, I take great pride in those four years I supported myself and earned career recognition. I'm glad I was able to marry a man *not* by necessity—because I needed financial support—but by choice. Knowing I could find a job again if my family ever needs the income brings me great comfort. After all, none of us know what the future holds.

I believe all girls should live on their own at least a few years before tying the knot. Besides building character and self-esteem, this teaches you the value of a dollar. Money takes on a new meaning when you alone have to earn it, and while it's easy to blow through someone else's wallet (think of your parents, and how quickly you'll spend *their* money), blowing through your own is another story.

Dating is a healthy part of growing up when done correctly and at the right time. Spending time with different personalities helps you see what you do and don't like in the opposite sex. But when you find yourself growing serious with a boy, keep it in check. Don't invest so much in his needs that you neglect your own.

A healthy relationship will draw you closer to those who love you: God, your family, and your friends. It will boost your confidence as you work toward goals. A healthy relationship will *not* do the following things:

- Isolate you from friends or family because you're ditching them to be with him
- Cause your grades to slip because you're out on the town when you should be studying
- Fill you with self-doubt
- Put you on an emotional roller coaster

As I mentioned, your relationship almost certainly will end. So think about how you'll feel when that happens.

- Will you resent the time you poured into your boyfriend— or be thankful he made you a better person?
- Will you regret getting sidetracked from your goals—or say he encouraged you like you encouraged him?
- Will the break-up feel like the end of the world—or will it end amicably, leaving the door open for a future friendship?

- Will you be ashamed of how you engaged sexually—or thankful you held back in moments of temptation, saving your body for your husband?

Whoever he is, he isn't worth obsessing over. He isn't worth the attention he takes away from your life purpose. Please don't sell yourself short or believe your most important contribution to this world is keeping a boy happy. God's plan for you aims way higher than that. A boy may be part of your plan, but he will never be *The Plan*.

You have a role in building God's kingdom. It's up to you to use your resources and notice the opportunities God places on your path. Yes, a boy can enhance your life tremendously, but he'll never complete you. Only Christ can complete you, and if you want to make investments you won't regret, invest in things that ultimately serve Him.

"DO NOT CONFORM TO THE PATTERN OF THIS WORLD, BUT BE TRANSFORMED BY THE RENEWING OF YOUR MIND. THEN YOU WILL BE ABLE TO TEST AND APPROVE WHAT GOD'S WILL IS—HIS GOOD, PLEASING AND PERFECT WILL."

(ROMANS 12:2)

THERE ARE GIRLS BOYS *DATE* AND GIRLS BOYS *MARRY*

What a boy wants at age sixteen is different from what he'll want at twenty-six. So if you want him long term, do not be the short term.

At sixteen, he's not looking for everlasting love. He's not thinking about soul mates. Even if he entertains notions of marriage with you, marriage is not the primary topic on a boy's mind. What is? Well, let me shoot it to you straight:

SEX.

Sex, sex, sex. That is what boys your age primarily think about, even if it may be the *last* thing on your mind. It is what they talk about too, which is why anything you do with a boy *won't* be kept confidential. He may be trustworthy while you date, but once you break up, all bets are off. *I'm not condoning this behavior, but I want you to know it happens.* The boy you thought was a steel vault may become an open book as he shares your intimate secrets with friends—or worse yet, a locker room full of jocks.

You know how it's hard for girls not to gossip, how it just *happens* when you're together? Well, pull some guys together and their lips get loose too. Besides talking about sex, guys trade information on girls. They share any scoop they have: what girls are easy, what girls aren't, who sleeps around, who won't. Discussing sexual conquests is a frequent topic of conversation for boys. Many try to prove their manhood by bragging about who can't resist them.

It's immature and rude to behave this way, but I'm letting you know that it happens, and you'd be wise to remember this when you are making decisions about dating.

In the locker room, stories really tend to get embellished. Guys often one-up each other to enhance their image. As one father I know told his teenage daughter, "Whatever you really do, it will get exaggerated in the locker room. So if you kiss him, he'll tell everyone he touched your breasts."

Consider yourself warned, my friend.

Am I saying all boys are jerks? That you might as well write them off now? No. What I'm saying is that teenage boys have a lot of growing up to do. And honestly, so do teenage girls. God is working on the boys just like He's working on you. Many boys (but not all) will make great progress in the next ten to fifteen years. They'll mature and become good men with stable jobs and a desire to provide for others, including their wife and children.

But right now, boys are after a good time. They're having sexual thoughts that would make your cheeks blaze with embarrassment. Even "nice guys" fight internal battles with their sex drive. They've been raised to treat women with respect. They know it's their duty to protect a girl's purity. Yet when they're attracted to a girl, their minds get lustful. They want to act on their desires, not wrestle with them. They want to forget what they *should* do and do what feels right.

Teenage boys are naturally inclined to be aggressive, so what do you think happens when you add promiscuous, aggressive females to the mix? Lots and lots of sex, right? A hook-up culture like what we see today?

Sadly, that is the dating scene you're dealing with. On one side you have oversexed boys with raging hormones. On the other side are girls willing to feed the beast. For every boy who's after a good time, there are three females lined up to give him one, oftentimes because they have low self-esteem or other issues that mistakenly lead them to believe that sex will translate into love. Fueling the fire has never been easier.

It isn't one sex corrupting the other; it is both genders corrupting each other. Instead of seeing each other as brothers and sisters in Christ, teenage boys and girls often use each other for personal motives and pleasures. Then they wonder why they can't get respect or settle into a healthy relationship.

God didn't create sex to be used this way. He didn't create it for teenagers who fall madly in love and plan to get married one day, either. God created sex for *marriage*, and when shared between a husband and wife, it's wonderful and holy. But take sex out of its proper context and problems abound.

Without the commitment of marriage, that promise before God, sex will make you more insecure and clingy. You'll get emotionally attached even if you agree to "no strings attached." It is impossible *not* to get attached, because no amount of willpower can keep your heart from getting involved. What you do with your body affects your heart and soul. Sex outside of marriage creates scars that stay with you forever.

So what am I suggesting you do? I'm suggesting you remember that Donna Greene story about the young men at the wedding, because it's a great illustration of how most boys change over time. While some men never mature and will never acquire a responsible mind-set toward women and sex, the guys worth having in your life *will* evolve. They'll become men you can imagine following to the ends of the earth because their love for you is as genuine and selfless as your love for them.

They'll still have a sex drive. They'll still consider physical attraction very important. They'll still want a girl who is fun and makes them happy. But also factoring into their dating choices will be considerations like these:

- Could I marry this girl? Do I want to grow old together?
- Can I imagine her as the mother of my children? Is she the role model I want for my daughters and sons?
- Does she make me a better person? Am I happiest when I'm with her?
- Do we connect spiritually? Does that spiritual connection deepen our physical connection? Does she believe in God, and will she help me create a faithful home?
- What do my friends and family think of her? What is my mother's verdict?

- Will she be an asset to my career? Will I be proud to introduce her to my boss and co-workers?
- Do our dreams align, and will we be able to help each other reach them?
- Do I love her more than anyone on earth?
- If she gets away, will I regret it forever?

Come marrying time, guys worth having set high standards. A girl who got overlooked in high school or college may suddenly be considered the ideal mate. Guys may date the fun girl, but they want to marry the package—someone who is smart, pretty, kind, real, fun, confident, and overall amazing. They want the girl who wasn't conquered by every boy and his brother, whose name wasn't dragged through mud during locker room dialogue.

Likewise, girls should also have high expectations for their future spouse. You deserve a man who has held himself to the same standards you have.

Make good choices now, and you'll be much more likely to have good men interested in marrying you later. Don't worry if boys aren't beating down your door or begging for dates. Consider it a blessing if they choose the wild girls over you. To me that's a sign you're on the right track. Stay true to yourself and a path God can bless, and eventually the boys worth having (those who respect you and your virtues) will come around.

REMEMBER: YOU'RE A WOMAN OF GOD

We covered a lot of ground regarding boys, dating, marriage, and sex. Here are some final thoughts:

1. Chasing boys may capture their attention, but it won't capture their heart.

God wired boys to be the pursuer, not the pursued. He wants them to take the lead because it cultivates them into young men. It prepares them for their future roles as husbands, providers, and leaders of the home. You aren't doing boys a favor by taking the risk of rejection off them; you're depriving them of an experience that helps them grow up and mature.

Guys take pleasure in the pursuit, and if they're attracted to you, they'll go after you. You can't force chemistry, nor will you "grow" on anyone by being pushy. A boy either is or isn't attracted to you. This is also true for girls, of course, as even the best laid plans from a persistent boy can't make you like him, right?

The way a relationship begins sets the tone. So if you start in role reversal, catching your heart's desire by chasing him, expect to continue taking the lead. Don't count on your boyfriend to court you, plan special dates, or initiate contact. Don't be surprised if he is passive and lukewarm in his feelings toward you. The reason teenage boys are often lazy daters is because they can be. Why ask girls out when girls will ask them? Why make dinner reservations when your girlfriend agrees to meet up with friends and count it as a "date"?

If you want a boy to court you, don't make it too easy. Let him work a little, because a guy worth having will rise to the challenge. I'm *not* telling you to play hard to get or mess with a boy's mind. I'm simply suggesting that you set reasonable standards. If a boy wants a date, have him pick you up and meet your parents. If he calls you Friday afternoon to go out Friday night, be wary if this becomes a pattern. A real date should be planned several days in advance, not thrown together as an afterthought—or after someone else cancelled on him.

Remember, you're a woman of God. And by making your life rich and fulfilling before a boy enters the picture, boys (and girls) will long to be part of your world.

2. *Pure relationships allow you to stay friendly with your exes. You never know who will reenter your life.*

A guy I know lives in the same community with two ex-girlfriends. All three of them have children the same age, so their paths cross a lot.

He's remained good friends with one ex-girlfriend because their relationship was short and innocent. His son and her daughter are close friends, and their families hang out together. But with his second ex-girlfriend, he can't interact like that because their relationship was heavy and sexual. They were best friends before they dated, so when they broke up, he lost his best friend.

While everyone is happily married, the awkwardness remains. Once you cross certain lines with boys, there's no going back. Even twenty, thirty, or forty years later, the memories linger. Staying mindful of this may help you think twice before getting physical.

3. Dating is about selectivity, not settling.

The purpose of dating is to find the *one person* you want to marry. Selectivity is the name of the game as you and the boys you date discover what you do and don't like in the opposite sex. This is a time to find out if you and your date have the same values and goals in life.

With some boys, you'll know immediately whether you're compatible. There may be one date—and that's it. With other boys, you'll want to dig deeper. You may date a few months to explore the potential.

Over time, you'll uncover qualities that aren't readily apparent. You may decide, "I love how he always treats me like a lady. I want that in a husband," or, "I need more affection. He won't even hold my hand in public. My husband has to be affectionate."

Through dating and friendships with the opposite sex, you discern the qualities you like. You learn how to interact with boys and build a radar for those you can trust (the protectors) and those you can't (the predators). After many years of this, you gain clarity of what you're looking for in a life partner so that when you finally meet your husband, you're ready.

4. Purity is a choice you won't regret.

Your future husband is out there. He may be three minutes away or three thousand miles across the country, going about life like you.

One day, when you two get serious and start talking about marriage, you'll need to share intimate details about your past. He'll give you the breakdown on his, and you'll do the same. This could be a hard conversation. There could be hurt feelings and tears as confessions about old flames and flings get laid on the table for you or him to come to terms with.

As difficult as this conversation may be, it's necessary. A marriage deserves full honesty, and keeping secrets isn't fair to your spouse. Secrets have a way of revealing themselves in time, and hiding yours will only cause more harm and feelings of betrayal when the truth emerges.

The choices you make with boys are *not* carried to your grave; they're carried into your marriage. When the time comes for your big conversation, I want you to feel proud. I want you to watch your husband's face light up because you just told him how you've saved the sacred gift of your body for him alone.

The boys you date now won't be your spouse. They're meant to lead you to your spouse, just as you'll help lead them to theirs. Your best dating approach is to treat them like you hope some girl is treating your future husband—as his guardian, not his lover. By protecting your purity *and* the purity of the boys you date, you'll grow closer than you ever could having sex.

While the boys may not appreciate that now, they will one day. So will their spouses. Love says, "I can wait." Lust says, "I have to have it now."

If you've had sex already, it isn't too late to change. Confess your sins and let God's grace and forgiveness make you new. Ask God to help you stay pure. Remember, He'll give you a way out whenever you're tempted (1 Corinthians 10:13).

Be patient as you wait for Mr. Right. He isn't marriage material yet because God is working on him just as He's working on you. Seek God's will for *your life*, develop *your potential*, and keep boys in the proper perspective.

When you focus on bettering yourself, you don't need to chase boys because eventually, the right boy will find you.

DISCUSSION QUESTIONS

1. Have you ever put a dream on hold for a boy? Do you ever make sacrifices—like helping your boyfriend with a class project when you really need to study for a test—that ultimately hurt you?

2. Do girls at your school chase boys? If so, what are your thoughts? Based on your observations, do you see a difference between relationships led by boys versus those led by girls?

3. Do you believe sex should be saved for marriage? If so, have you made a conscious commitment to protect your purity even when you fall in love?

4. Why do guys make good friends? What can they offer that girlfriends can't? What do you like about the opposite sex? What do you dislike?

5. How might teen culture change if everyone treated each other as brothers and sisters in Christ? If a boy protected your purity by holding back on his sexual urges, would you consider him backward or trustworthy? Would it weaken your relationship or strengthen it?

Chapter 5

Self-Worship

Truth #6: You weren't made to worship yourself.

I knew I was overreacting, but I couldn't stop. The sight of my father triggered a meltdown.

I was in college and taking two courses in summer school. For most students, summer school was an excuse to stay on campus and have fun. You intentionally signed up for easy classes, because who wants to study during summer?

The history class I had selected sounded fine on paper, but in reality it was a nightmare. The teacher was arrogant and prided himself on rarely giving As. Being an A student, I thought I'd be an exception. I knew it wouldn't be easy to sacrifice nights out with my friends to stay in and study, but I was willing to do it.

After all, my GPA was everything to me. It was my baby, the one thing I'd throw my body in front of a speeding car for in order to save it.

I needed money, and since my parents lived near campus, my dad agreed to meet me outside the fitness facility where he exercised. I'd just received bad news from my professor, news I didn't plan to share. I was too embarrassed and ashamed.

My father lit up when he saw me. He hugged me, kissed my forehead, and said he'd missed me. As he withdrew cash from his wallet, my defenses weakened, and all my emotions broke loose. The tears I'd held back since leaving history class twenty minutes earlier came out in a rush.

"Honey, what's the matter?" my father asked as I fell to pieces. I couldn't look at him. I couldn't breathe. I couldn't speak or think. The weight of disappointment in my chest was heavy. I was *crushed*.

My father held me as I cried. Even in my hysteria, I felt bad about the scenarios probably going through his mind as he wondered why his twenty-year-old daughter was distraught. But Dad didn't look scared. He didn't seem to dread what I might say. Whatever my problem was, I knew he'd accept it and love me the same. That assurance gave me the courage to admit my failure.

In choking sobs I said, "I . . . got . . . a . . . B . . . on . . . my . . . history test!"

I spit out the word B as if it were acid. To me, it certainly was. My history grade depended on two tests, and unless I made a perfect score the next time, I wouldn't get my A. My father smiled, hugged me tighter, and calmed me down. He repeated what he always said in these situations: "If you tried your hardest, there's nothing you could have done differently. All you can give is your best and ask God to take it from there."

My father knew I was tough on myself, and his antidote to my self-torment was always love and grace. My mother was the same way. They never pushed me to be more, do more, and achieve more, because I didn't need that. I put enough pressure on myself, and if they'd added more, I would have cracked.

And while I laugh at this story now—especially the absurdity of me treating a B as a fatality—it also saddens me. Because what my breakdown symbolized was my out of whack priorities.

In short, I idolized the wrong things. While it was good that I applied myself, I wasn't using my talents to glorify God. I was using my talents to glorify *me*, Kari Kubiszyn. I was building myself up, making a self-monument. And when a stone to that monument fell, the whole structure crumbled.

Many teenage girls battle the same problem I did: perfectionism. I wanted to be the perfect girl, and some days I could fool myself into believing I came close. But really, my perfectionism was self-worship. It focused my attention on *me* instead of *God*. I believe I missed out on many spiritual encounters because my eyes weren't open to His presence. I struggled with insecurity and doubt because I stored my confidence in the wrong places.

Girls who self-worship aren't just those who strut around in tiaras, bragging about their greatness, their beauty, and their superiority. In some form, we're all guilty of self-worship. We all create a false idol of ourselves, breaking the first and most important commandment: "I am the LORD your God. . . . You shall have no other gods before me" (Exodus 20:2–3).

Take it from a girl who's been there: self-worship is a waste of time. It distracts you from the One who truly matters. Only when you step off the pedestal and let Jesus fill your heart can you enjoy true happiness.

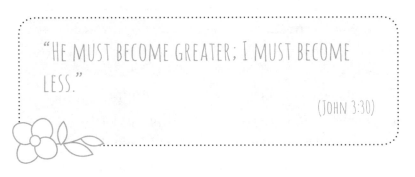

"HE MUST BECOME GREATER; I MUST BECOME LESS."

(JOHN 3:30)

YOUR LIFE IS *NOT* ABOUT YOU

The word of the year in 2013 was *selfie*. The *Oxford English Dictionary* chose *selfie* as the runaway winner because use of the word rose 17,000 percent during the year.[4]

A selfie is a self-portrait taken with a smart phone or webcam and shared on social media. I've taken selfies with family and friends, and you probably have too. Done appropriately and not overused, they can be fun.

But it's worth noting what the explosive trend of selfies reveals about our culture. In short, we're more narcissistic than ever. We've become hooked on seeking praise, attention, and validation online. Thanks to the Internet, we can find instant applause and sometimes fame. Just *one* picture with a lot of "likes" can get you noticed. Just *one* video going viral can make you an overnight sensation.

Isn't that enticing? Deep down, wouldn't most of us like to be celebrities? If you're like many teenage girls, you may have dreamed of catching your big break online, being discovered as a singer, model, dancer, actress, fashion designer, etc. Maybe you don't care *what* you get famous for as long as you're famous.

But let's think about how God views our self-promotion. What does He think about our building identities online and not through Christ? Does God love you more if you're the Internet darling and less if you're the laughingstock? Does He approve of how mean and rude people can be in the virtual world because mean and rude attract attention and make people laugh sometimes?

You know the answers. You know it's a slippery slope to base your self-esteem on the acceptance or rejection of others. You've seen how fickle people can be, loving you one minute, criticizing you the next. Yet despite this, you listen to what others say and let it get to you. While their praise goes to your head, their criticism goes to your heart.

Aren't you tired of the emotional roller coaster? Wouldn't

you like to feel good about yourself *consistently*? Wouldn't you love a healthy self-image that isn't volatile and overly sensitive to public opinion?

What you should know is this: *you weren't made to worship yourself.* You weren't made to base your identity on the world's fluctuating opinion of you or your opinion of yourself.

God designed you to find your identity in Christ. Through that relationship, you discover God. You receive extravagant love, grace, and acceptance. Even on your worst days, God loves you at full capacity. *Nothing* changes His love.

Isn't that refreshing? Aren't you relieved to know that the Father who knows you best—with all your flaws and sinfulness—also loves you best? For *Him* to be so taken, you must be special.

Since God is truth, He sees the truth about you. And if you want to discover that truth, learn to see yourself through His eyes. Begin by understanding three things:

1. The difference between self-love and self-worship
2. The need for gratitude and humility
3. Your place in the universe

SELF-LOVE VERSUS SELF-WORSHIP

Self-love is derived from God. It is kind, gentle, and forgiving. You see yourself first and foremost as God's child, holding up a mirror to the Holy Spirit inside you. Since God's strength is made perfect in weakness (2 Corinthians 12:9), your imperfections are seen as opportunities for His grace to shine.

Self-love focuses on your inherent worth and beauty. It understands how the negative, critical voice in your head is not the voice of God; it's the voice of Satan. When you love yourself, you find value in WHOSE you are, not WHO you are.

Self-worship is derived from the world. It masquerades as self-love through thoughts like this:

I'm fabulous and amazing.

People love me and envy my life.

I'm better than most people and destined for greatness.

If I work hard, God will make my dreams come true.

When you self-worship, you look out for yourself. Others become competition and threats. You're ashamed of your imperfections and inadequacies, so you hide them. You believe if anyone knew your weak points, they'd exploit them or quit liking you.

Failure is unacceptable when you self-worship. You're happy when life is good and miserable when it isn't. You love yourself at your best, yet hate yourself at your worst.

It's easy to confuse self-love and self-worship in our culture of girl power. Both encourage you to be brave, bold, and confident. Both tell you to dream big and trust yourself because you're stronger and more capable than you think.

But one key difference between the two is *who* gets credit. Are your achievements yours alone, or is God working through you? To find out where you fall on the self-love/self-worship spectrum, consider these questions:

- Do you put your faith in *yourself* or *God*?
- Are you seeking approval from the *world* or *God*?
- Do you consider your talents to be *naturally there* or *God-given*?
- When you tap your inner strength, are you tapping into *yourself* or the *Holy Spirit*?
- Does your life glorify *you* or *God*?
- Are your life blessings *earned* by good deeds and moral living, or are they *undeserved gifts* from above?

The fact is, you and I are helpless without God. Only by His grace can we function. What seem like basic abilities—walking, seeing, hearing—are really miracles because God has allowed them in our lives. Tomorrow we could wake up without these abilities. *There is no guarantee.*

Understanding this makes you grateful. It helps you appreciate God. Admitting dependency doesn't show weakness; it shows growth. It means you "get it."

All the good things in your life come from God—doors that open at *exactly* the right moment, people who help you through hard times, opportunities that suddenly appear. Nothing is an accident, and even in terrible circumstances, God blesses you. As you open your eyes to this truth, it becomes evident.

How you use your gifts is a choice. Are you looking to build a personal empire or God's kingdom? When you choose God, you use your gifts to serve. You follow Christ's example of selfless love.

It's impossible to be selfish and truly happy. It's impossible to live in God's light when you distance yourself through self-worship. Whether you realize it or not, you and God are a team. Without Him, you're completely incapable.

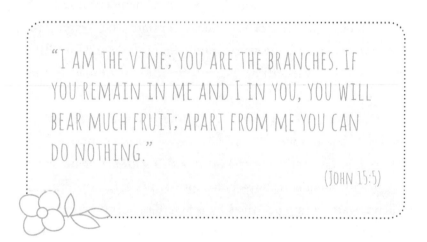

"I AM THE VINE; YOU ARE THE BRANCHES. IF YOU REMAIN IN ME AND I IN YOU, YOU WILL BEAR MUCH FRUIT; APART FROM ME YOU CAN DO NOTHING."

(JOHN 15:5)

GRATITUDE AND HUMILITY: KEEPING YOU IN CHECK

Remember what I said about letting the praise of others go to your head and the criticism go to your heart?

Well, let me confess: *I am guilty*. I struggle to keep a proper attitude toward myself. Although I know better, I often put too much weight in the world's opinion and too little in God's.

On one end, I beat myself up. I dwell on the mistakes I've

made or the people I've let down even after I've asked for forgiveness. I listen to the critic in my head (Satan's voice) and get so down on myself I can't see my own good. When I'm in a self-destructive mode, I have to dig deep and pray hard. Only God can pull me through.

On the other end, I get big-headed. I can let a compliment or triumph inflate my ego and fill my mind with thoughts of *me, me, me.* In my self-consumption, I forget about serving. I lose sight of the world at large because my attention is focused inward.

Two things help me stay grounded: gratitude and humility. When these virtues fill my heart, I grow resilient to swinging emotions.

Gratitude isn't just for Thanksgiving; it's a habit we're called to practice year-round. There is always a reason to praise God. There is always a silver lining or something to sustain hope.

Think outside the box when expressing your thankfulness. Turn negatives into positives by replacing feelings with truth. Use God's promises as affirmation, as shown below, and write them on sticky notes you can post on your mirror when you need a quick of reference of truth:

- I may not like my reflection in the mirror right now, but I'll praise God because I'm fearfully and wonderfully made (Psalm 139:14).
- I may be sad because all my friends have boyfriends and I don't, but I will praise God because He has plans for my future (Jeremiah 29:11).

- I may think I'm unlovable because I've comm horrible sin, but I'll remember no height and can separate me from the love of God that is in ... son Christ Jesus (Romans 8:39).
- I may hate cleaning house because my mom is sick, but I'll do it with all my heart, as if I'm working for God, not man (Colossians 3:23).
- I may be scared to stand up for the girl our entire school is badmouthing, but I will because there's no greater love than laying down your life for your friend (John 15:13).
- I may be hurt and embarrassed by the lies being spread about me, but I will trust that what man means for evil, God can use for good (Genesis 50:20).
- I may be mad at God because my father's been diagnosed with terminal cancer, but I will trust the Lord with all my heart, and lean not on my own understanding (Proverbs 3:5–6).
- I may be miserable in this rough patch, but I'll seek joy during this trial because the testing of my faith develops perseverance, and perseverance helps me mature into the image of Christ (James 1:2–4).

To be grateful, you need humility. Humility keeps you aware that you are *no better* and *no worse* than anyone else. It prevents you from being overly affected by events, good or bad. When you're humble, you stay off the emotional roller coaster because you live by these basic truths:

- "I am God's child."
- "He loves me always."
- "Even if I lose everything, I lose nothing since I still have eternal life through Christ."
- "I live for heaven's rewards, not earthly rewards. No suffering or disappointment in this life can take away my hope in the afterlife."

The opposite of humility is pride. And of all the evils, pride is the worst because it separates you from God's virtues. Humility, on the other hand, draws you into God's will. It helps you discover your role in the great show God is running. Being humble doesn't make you meek or cowardly; it makes you strong and fearless. It helps you recognize who you are before God and what He created you to do.

The Creator of the universe also controls the universe. Whatever light you shine, direct the beam toward Him.

"IN THE SAME WAY, LET YOUR LIGHT SHINE BEFORE OTHERS, THAT THEY MAY SEE YOUR GOOD DEEDS AND GLORIFY YOUR FATHER IN HEAVEN."
(MATTHEW 5:16)

YOUR PLACE IN THE UNIVERSE

There's a popular phrase I often see on journals for girls. Whenever I catch it, it always makes me pause:

IT'S ALL ABOUT ME

Now, I love journals, and I'm all for products that celebrate girls and encourage self-reflection. But what bothers me about *It's All About Me* is that it's misleading and wrong.

It's *not* all about you (or me). Yes, you're important, but you're not the center of the universe. And writing about yourself for three hundred pages, focusing only on *your* feelings, *your* thoughts, and *your* life . . . well, it tends to lead to self-centered thinking.

Perhaps a better journal would be: *Getting Over Myself.* You'd still write about your strengths, weaknesses, passions, and fears, but for the purpose of serving God better. In *Getting Over Myself,* you'd focus on the big picture. You'd joyfully admit your small-ness in God's master plan and reflect on finding your relevance in God's great creation.

Discovering yourself this way for three hundred pages would cultivate selfless thinking. And selfless thinking, as surprising as this may sound, cultivates joy.

What's the Root of Your Self-Worth?

All of us have areas of life that build us up,

strong points we're known for among family and friends.

These areas, even when they're good, can become a god. Whatever distinguishes you from the crowd is easy to obsess over because it boosts your self-esteem. It may become the thing you turn to for reassurance when you're doubting yourself and need to feel better.

So I ask you: What fuels your confidence? What external factors do you base your identify on? If you lost them tomorrow, could you handle it?

External factors may include the following:

- Your appearance (always looking good, outshining other girls)
- Your performance (excelling in school, sports, the arts, etc.)
- Your relationships (dating popular boys, having the right friends)
- Your body (an enviable physique)
- Your wardrobe (the latest and greatest fashions)
- Your lifestyle (a lavish upbringing and parents who spoil you rotten)
- Your accomplishments (titles, trophies, public recognition)

Recognizing the root of your self-worth is crucial. God wants you to make Jesus the root, to find your identity in Him and value yourself because you're God's child. *That* makes you special. Nothing you do or achieve adds more worth.

But the world we live in speaks differently. According to the world, your worth is based on your external scorecard. You're encouraged to be self-focused and make mini-gods of your looks, grades, relationships, fashion, accomplishments, etc. Living this way comes with a price, however. It sets you up for despair and breakdowns when your false gods fail you.

Eventually, they all do.

Overnight your boyfriend can (and will) dump you. Your friends can (and will) disappear. Your dad can lose his job, wiping out your lavish lifestyle. Your body can be scarred in an accident, and the new exchange student from Spain can replace you as the school bombshell.

Even your talents can let you down. You may lose the championship for your volleyball team or wake up tomorrow without your gifts. Only by God's daily grace do you have them in the first place.

But if your confidence is rooted in Jesus, nothing breaks you. Your external world can collapse and you'll still be standing. By putting your faith in the right basket, you can live fearlessly. Earthly trappings hold no power over you.

Once you have *that* confidence, God can use you to move mountains.

"I AM NOT SAYING THIS BECAUSE I AM IN NEED, FOR I HAVE LEARNED TO BE CONTENT WHATEVER THE CIRCUMSTANCES. I KNOW WHAT IT IS TO BE IN NEED, AND I KNOW WHAT IT IS TO HAVE PLENTY. I HAVE LEARNED THE SECRET OF BEING CONTENT IN ANY AND EVERY SITUATION, WHETHER WELL FED OR HUNGRY, WHETHER LIVING IN PLENTY OR IN WANT. I CAN DO ALL THIS THROUGH HIM WHO GIVES ME STRENGTH."

(PHILIPPIANS 4:11–13)

JOY: JESUS, OTHERS, YOURSELF

Your greatest call in life is to love others.

You can achieve your wildest dreams, but if you fail to love, you've failed at life.

Love puts the needs of others first. It shows kindness and respect, not to win popularity contests, but because kindness and respect reveal God's mercy and goodness to others. It passes on the grace you've received.

Love doesn't keep score. It doesn't expect payback. It doesn't have hidden agendas or use people. Since you may use someone without realizing it, it's important to consider the *motive* behind your actions. Ask yourself, "Why am I doing this? Am I passing on God's love, or am I trying to earn favor from this person?"

It's human nature to assume our motives are all good, so ask God for clarity. Pray for help in seeing the true state of your heart. *Only when your motives are pure can you love others properly and serve God.*

We're all selfish by nature. We all put desires of our body over desires in our soul because it's an easier way to live. But when you live for the instant gratification of your body, you empty your soul. You starve yourself spiritually.

Jesus is the solution to selfishness. By putting Him first, others second, and yourself third, you align your heart with God's. Only then can you build monuments for God's kingdom that count. Only then can you be saved from the self-worship that feels good in the moment but ultimately destroys you.

DISCUSSION QUESTIONS

1. What idols do you put before God? What has such a hold on you that if you lost it tomorrow, you might question God's goodness?

2. Does social media affect your self-esteem? Do you ever base your self-worth on how many "likes" you get or post selfies to draw compliments?

3. Are you grateful, or do you tend to complain? What problem in your life has a silver lining you can praise God for?

4. Imagine waking up tomorrow with nothing: no friends, no family, no home, no material possessions. Could you find joy in the one thing *nobody* can take away, your identity in Christ?

5. Do you ever show kindness so others will owe you? What does God think about secret motives like that? Why do they prevent you from loving others?

Chapter 6

Perseverance

Truth #5: People peak at different times in life.
Trust God's plan for you.

A friend of mine from high school recently shared a video called *The Man and the Butterfly*.[5]

It's about a man who finds a cocoon and watches for hours as the butterfly struggles to fit through the cocoon's tiny hole. When the butterfly stops making progress and looks as if he'll go no farther, the man decides to help. Using scissors, he snips away the cocoon and sets the butterfly free.

The butterfly emerges easily, but its body is swollen and its wings are small and shriveled. The man keeps watching, expecting the wings to enlarge and support the butterfly's body, but they don't. The butterfly spends the rest of its life crawling on the ground, never realizing its potential.

What the man didn't realize is that the butterfly needed a longer struggle to strengthen its wings. Both the tight cocoon and the work required to push through the tiny opening are God's way of forcing fluid from its body to get the butterfly's wings ready for flight. *By "helping" the butterfly, the man actually crippled it.* He opened the cocoon too early, depriving the butterfly of the opportunity to develop skills he'd need to survive.

Do you ever wish your life was easier? Have you ever felt *stuck* inside your cocoon? Have you ever wondered if God deserted you by allowing pain and suffering? If someone offered you a shortcut out of your cocoon, a quick and easy escape, would you take it even if it fundamentally changed who you are forever?

In terms of freedom, are you so ready to feel the wind beneath your wings you can barely stand it sometimes?

If you answered "yes" to these questions, you're normal. Nobody likes to struggle. Nobody likes to be stuck. Nobody likes to wait for good things to happen. Given the choice, we'd all take shortcuts out of our cocoon. We'd all cut corners and find freedom on *our* terms.

But following God means trusting that every obstacle serves a purpose. If God removed a challenge you're facing right now, you might not be prepared for what He's planned. Your wings wouldn't be strong enough to fly. Regardless of how your struggles may appear, they aren't a waste of time. God works all things together for the good of those who love Him (Romans 8:28), and having faith means trusting that.

Only when you push through life's *impossibly small holes* do you understand how much you need God and how miraculous your life can be through Him.

God's plan for you has perfect timing. Even when you feel neglected or forgotten, His plan is in motion. He's bringing people and circumstances into your life that will enable you to later break free and fly. Forcing your cocoon open too soon messes with God's timing. Quitting or taking the easy way out prevents you from developing the character, endurance, and resilience you will need to handle the real world.

When you leave your cocoon, your life will still be hard. You will face ups and downs, seasons where you fly and seasons where you crawl. And while you can't always avoid the dips, you can learn to cope. You can see them for what they are—growth opportunities—and become a better person by using your downtime to reflect and regroup.

What happens while you're waiting is often more important than what you're waiting for. God cares more about the person you're becoming than anything you achieve. For Him it's about the process, not the results.

I hope you find comfort in that. I hope you find freedom in knowing that every trial you experience prepares you for what's to come.

> "AND ENDURANCE DEVELOPS STRENGTH OF CHARACTER, AND CHARACTER STRENGTHENS OUR CONFIDENT HOPE OF SALVATION."
>
> (ROMANS 5:4)

YOU DON'T WANT TO PEAK IN HIGH SCHOOL

When I was growing up, I came in second place a lot.

In many organizations, I was elected vice president. In two high school beauty walks, I was named first runner-up. Committee heads often asked me to co-chair. And while my grades were high, I was never in the top tier of students with high standardized test scores and scholarships galore.

I was grateful for my opportunities, but deep down I wondered if I had a defect. I wondered if this would be my life theme forever—my giving 110 percent and coming in second best. For just one day or one night, I wanted to *win*. I wanted to rise above the crowd and receive the top accolades.

It never happened, and life went on. My mother, who understood my frustration, would sometimes say, "You'll peak later in life, Kari. You'll get better and better with age."

She meant this as a compliment, explaining how some

people peak too young and fizzle, never reaching the same high again. And while I appreciated Mom's faith in me, I still thought I had a defect. I suspected something must be seriously wrong with me.

Today, I can laugh at my "runner-up" insecurities. I'm thankful I have stories of highs *and* lows to share with my daughters and now *you*. My mother was right—my life has gotten better with time, not because I win more, necessarily, but because I found my true callings later in life as a wife, mother, and writer. This stage I'm in "clicks" for me.

And while I loved high school and college, I'm happiest where I am now. My best days aren't behind me; they're in front of me and still ahead. A peak, I now realize, goes beyond accomplishments, spotlights, and moments of glory. A peak can mean different things to different to people, but to me it means the following:

- *Strong, loving relationships*
- *Work that matters*
- *A full heart*
- *A happy home*
- *Self-confidence and purposeful living*
- *Intimacy with God*

What you should know is this: *People peak at different times of life. And if you're not peaking now, that really is okay.*

You don't want to be the girl who peaks in high school—or

junior high or college for that matter—but crashes when real life kicks in.

I'm not saying the girl who is Miss Everything at your school is doomed. Plenty of young stars have lives that improve with time because they have the substance and smarts to keep growing. But oftentimes, life outside the high school cocoon is disappointing for Miss Everything because suddenly she's a small fish in a big sea. Her charmed life is over.

Imagine if you'd always been the center of attention. If you never had to share the spotlight, and if everyone treated you like a queen, doing anything you said. Wouldn't you be more self-centered than your peers? Wouldn't your self-perception and sense of reality be a little warped? Don't you think it'd be a rude awakening to discover—WHAM!—life won't always work in your favor, and you're not more special than everyone else after all?

Think about all the Hollywood starlets who crash and burn because they have no limits, no one telling them no, and no spiritual path to keep them centered as they get everything they want at a young age and lose sight of what's important.

Yes, being Miss Everything has perks, but there is a flip side. Being catered to doesn't strengthen your wings. It doesn't prepare you to cope with the humbling truth that nobody remains the center of the universe forever because this universe isn't about *us*, it's about God. It doesn't teach you how to root for your friends when their life is up and yours is down.

When you're Miss Everything, you don't want life to change. And that's the problem—it *will* change. Whatever record you set, someone will break it. Whatever title you win, someone will replace you.

How well you roll with the punches depends on the hype you believe about yourself. If your success goes to your head, letting go of the past will be hard. If you enjoy your success while it lasts but never define yourself by it, you'll be humble enough to handle any circumstances that follow.

I want you to have fun. I want you to *feel* like these are the best days of your life because your friends are awesome and you can't fathom life without them.

After all, who else has seen you through the nitty-gritty rawness of growing up: buck teeth, braces, training bras, crushes, acne, puppy love, boyfriends, breakups, heartache, and most embarrassing moments?

Who else knows how weird your family can be?

Who else remembers how you barely survived geometry?

Who else witnessed that awkward phase you went through—and promises not to mention it again?

This roller coaster of "firsts" you're riding can be stressful yet magical. Whoever takes these loops with you, you're bonded for life. Only your earliest friends will know the 1.0 version of you, and that's why these friends are special. They see your "before" and watch you change from there.

Because if you live correctly, you won't stay at 1.0. You'll get better, smarter, and more capable each year. You'll broaden your horizons and discover parts of you that bring you closer to your ultimate design.

Girls who peak too early never make it past version 1.0, 2.0, or 3.0 of themselves. They don't grow, adapt, and mature. What's important in high school is not what's important in life, so don't lose hope if you haven't found your sweet spot yet. Listen for God's voice in your life and follow it, because in due time your day in the sun will come.

> "'FOR I KNOW THE PLANS I HAVE FOR YOU,' DECLARES THE LORD, 'PLANS TO PROSPER YOU AND NOT TO HARM YOU, PLANS TO GIVE YOU HOPE AND A FUTURE.'"
>
> (JEREMIAH 29:11)

FAILURE ISN'T THE END OF YOUR STORY— IT'S PART OF YOUR STORY

It took me seven years of committed writing to get a book deal. Seven years! That's a long time to wait for a dream to come true, right?

The good news is, it happened with this book. While I never expected my journey to published author to take seven years, I'm happy my first "baby" to enter the marketplace is for girls because girls are my comfort zone. I grew up with three sisters, I'm raising four daughters, and I know more amazing women than I can count.

My first writings were essays on motherhood. I thought they were great until every agent and publisher I queried rejected them. Unable to get my foot in the door through nonfiction, I switched to fiction. Fiction lit a fire in me, and over the course of five years, I wrote three novels.

I had a lot of bites with my fiction—agents requesting full manuscripts, one agent so interested I spent five months making revisions for her—but in the end no one wanted me. No one would take a chance on this diamond in the rough. Believing in myself when industry professionals didn't was tough. My sensitive soul wasn't prepared for that.

I wanted to quit sometimes. I wished for a different passion, one easier to break into than publishing. Deep down, however, I knew God wouldn't give me the gift of writing and a fire for it without a purpose. So instead of making my journey about me, I made it about Him. I found peace in limbo by reminding myself that as long as I'm pleasing God, I'm on the right track (Psalm 37:4).

I changed a lot during my seven-year wait, and so did my writing. As my spiritual life grew, I stopped trying to entertain readers and hoped to encourage them instead. Through my newspaper column and blog, I built a loyal following. I got enough positive feedback to know I wasn't wasting my time.

And then a few years ago, a junior high counselor friend

asked me to speak to her girls. Soon after we set a date, a tree fell on my family's house during a storm. It caused major damage and forced us to move out. I was so stressed I considered cancelling on my friend, but I wanted to keep my word. Even though the timing wasn't ideal, I knew I should follow through.

The speech went well, and when my friend invited me back a year later, I tweaked it and added stories. About six months after that, I needed a blog post, so I took that speech and created an article called "10 Truths Young Girls Should Know."

Immediately the article was a hit, going viral on Facebook and Pinterest. I'd never experienced such a tremendous response to anything I'd written. While I knew there was a market for a book, I decided I'd wait to write it because I was busy pitching my fiction work to literary agents.

Then two months after the excitement died down, I received an e-mail from an acquisitions editor. She'd seen my blog post and expressed interest in creating a book. For years I'd prayed for an opportunity like this, but never did I expect it to fall in my lap.

To be honest, that's not how my life works. When something good happens, it's typically because I chased it. To have someone *want* me and reach out without any initiative on my end was a strange yet wonderful sensation.

I share these details to illustrate how God works in mysterious ways. Even when He's quiet or when you think He's not listening, He's spinning wheels in motion behind the scenes. You have to trust that. Listen to the small voice inside you urging you to do the *next right thing*. What that voice suggests may seem irrelevant. You may wonder what the point is because it doesn't fit with your journey.

When my friend asked me to speak to her junior high girls, for instance, I saw no benefit to me. I know this is selfish, but one reason I almost backed out after the tree fell on my house was because I wasn't writing for teens at that time, I was writing for parents. Since these girls weren't my reader base and didn't live in my community, I doubted we'd ever cross paths again. I knew my friend would understand if I cancelled, yet for some reason, I felt a need to follow through. I considered it a chance to gain valuable experience.

What if I'd ignored that voice urging me to go? If I'd never written that speech, would I have written the blog post that led to this book? Probably not. What I thought was a favor to a friend was actually an opportunity in disguise. It was the genesis of something bigger to come.

In this world, there are people plans and there are God plans. The strategies humans employ to get ahead—connecting with connected people, hustling to get noticed, setting concrete goals—are not God's methods. While it's important to work hard and be ready when opportunity knocks, it's also crucial to be still and let God move (Psalm 46:10).

Leave space for God to surprise you. Watch Him fulfill the desires of your heart through unexpected channels. God plants people in your life for a reason. Don't discount anyone or burn bridges, because it may be the person you least expect who holds a key to your future. You never know what God has up His sleeve or what plot twists He'll use to carry out His will.

Will you go the extra mile to achieve your dreams? Will you let obstacles be an excuse to give up—or a chance to strengthen your wings?

Too many people let their obstacles win. They chase the dreams God's placed on their heart until it gets hard. Then they assume something must be wrong, because why else would there be impediments? But the truth is, life is difficult. And any dream worth having will have obstacles to separate those who are committed from those who are merely interested.

If you accept this now, challenges won't shock you. You can expect them and brace for them. Knowing obstacles are *normal* and nothing to take personally makes all the difference in whether you stick with your goals or abandon them.

Nobody's life is a constant mountaintop experience, because even wildly successful people have peaks *and* slumps. The two go together, and to see this concept illustrated, try drawing a mountain on paper. Notice the downward slopes on either side? Those represent your failures, rejections, and down times.

Failure isn't the end of your story—it's part of your story. It's the learning curve that leads to your next peak.

Your attitude determines your altitude. And if you consider failure shameful and something to avoid at all costs, you'll live in fear of it. You'll aim low and not challenge yourself. This may be safe, but it won't make you happy. Your peaks will be minimal and mildly gratifying. High peaks require high risk. The greater the risk, the greater the potential reward.

If, on the other hand, you see failure as a temporary dip that helps you grow and make better choices next time, it serves a purpose. It becomes a launching pad for your next peak. To rise up, you must push through the slump. You must persevere when you're most tempted to quit.

Will life get easier as you get older? Will you ever reach a point where you stay high all the time? Unfortunately, no. But you will stop seeing slumps as the end of the world. You will realize how they, too, are necessary to your story.

I know you're eager to make sense of life. You're hungry for reassurance that everything will be okay, that God will keep His promises to always be with you, never leaving you or forsaking you (Deuteronomy 31:6). But life can't be understood by looking ahead. If it could, you wouldn't need God. You'd have no incentive to walk with Him, no opportunities to earn His trust.

Faith is built when you let God carry you through hard times—and look *back* to recognize what He did. Only then, in hindsight, can the puzzle come together. That rejection from your school softball team? It led you to join a travel team that gave you more playing time and elevated your skills. That art show where you only sold one painting? Well, that one customer is now opening a restaurant, and she was so impressed by you that she's invited you to display and sell your work.

When the right door opens, you become *thankful* for things

that didn't pan out because if history had been different, you wouldn't have this moment. And when you praise God in the storm, or whenever there's a problem, you show you trust Him in advance. You turn the uncertainty of the present into hope for the future.

Do you trust God's plan for you? What about His timing? Do you believe that slumps can lead to peaks, failures can breed success, and trials can prepare you to fly?

If so, you have nothing to lose by trying. Even in the worst-case scenario—you fail—there's still hope for next time. So dream big, take risks, and keep the faith. Pour yourself into your heart's desire and God's will for you. Take on life's impossibly small holes like a butterfly pushing through a cocoon.

At the edge of your limits is where God's grace kicks in. That is where He performs miracles and shines brightest through you.

God sees your hard work, and He *will* reward your faithfulness. He knows the peaks He's planned for you, so as you wait for those peaks to arrive, praise God. Praise Him for the past, the present, and the future. Give thanks in all circumstances, for this is God's will for you in Christ (1 Thessalonians 5:18).

A grateful heart cultivates love for the Lord. As your heart for Him grows, so will your awareness of the beauty that exists in every high and low point of your journey.

DISCUSSION QUESTIONS

1. Using the "Man and the Butterfly" analogy, what stage are you in? Are you hiding in a cocoon, struggling to get out, or flying free?

2. What hard experiences made you a better person? Have you faced a difficulty that strengthened your wings?

3. How do you cope when you feel stuck, hopeless, or impatient with life? Do you get mad at God and write Him off, or do you pray and rely harder on your faith?

4. Do you believe God has a plan for you? Do you trust that He already knows every detail about your future—what job you'll have, who you'll marry, what you'll name your children—and is preparing you for what's ahead?

5. Why do you learn more from low points than high points? When you share your testimony of how God helped you survive a desert experience, how does it shape and influence the faith of others?

Chapter 7

Patience

veryone at school liked Gina. Even though she was a sophomore, the most popular juniors and seniors had started inviting her to their parties.

Gina's quick wit and warm personality were easy draws. She appealed to people at all levels of the social totem pole, from nerds and overachievers to cheerleaders and jocks.

Her best friends, Anne and Bentley, went to a few parties with her, but after being ignored all night by the stuck-up seniors, they swore they'd never go back. The popular crowd didn't take to them like they did Gina. Although no one said it, their company wasn't wanted.

When Gina got elected to the tenth-grade homecoming court, a senior named Mandy Jenkins—up for homecoming queen—took Gina under her wings. She invited Gina into her circle and arranged a shopping trip so they could find homecoming dresses together.

Gina couldn't decide what Mandy Jenkins saw in her, but the endorsement upped her rank in the popular crowd. When Mandy's best guy friend, John Wilson, asked Gina to homecoming so they could double date with Mandy and her boyfriend, Gina was ecstatic. John Wilson was the hottest guy in school! For years Gina had secretly crushed on him, and now this?

Gina couldn't wait to tell Anne and Bentley, but their reaction surprised her. "John Wilson is a *jerk*," they told her. "You're insane to go with him!" They also called Mandy two-faced and fake. It irritated Gina that they'd judge Mandy and John when they barely knew them. Maybe if they *tried* being nice, they'd see a different side.

Homecoming night was magical for Gina despite the tension with her best friends. The football team won by a landslide, Mandy was crowned homecoming queen, and Gina got treated like royalty. As her dad escorted her onto the field at halftime, he said he was proud of her. Gina loved seeing her father in good spirits. After losing his job, he rarely smiled anymore.

The post-game party for seniors was held at a farm outside

of town. There were no chaperones, of course—just kegs, hay, and a rowdy band you could hear a mile away.

When John left Gina's side to get drinks, she suddenly felt awkward. Everyone at the party was drinking, and half the girls were drunk already. Mandy had promised to stick by Gina, but when Gina glanced around, she saw Mandy dancing to the band and doing shots.

It hit Gina then how much she missed Anne and Bentley. If they were here, she wouldn't be the only one sober. The senior parties weren't uncomfortable when she'd had them to laugh with her at the maniacs losing control. But with her best friends and sidekicks gone, Gina grew insecure. She felt ridiculous standing alone like a stick in the mud, an outsider watching everyone else have fun.

John came back with two plastic cups spilling over with beer. The smell and foam on top almost made Gina gag. She didn't *want* to drink, but under these circumstances, she saw no choice. After all, she was stuck here for three hours. What was she supposed to do, spend the entire party being an outcast?

Maybe this will help me relax, Gina told herself as she took the cup. *Maybe I won't be so nervous around John and his friends.* Saying no at the senior parties was getting harder the more she came. She wanted people to like her and invite her back again.

Gina tried to take a sip, but she couldn't. Her stupid conscience was nagging her. Why couldn't this be an easy choice? Why did it seem like no matter what she did, she'd still feel awkward?

> "THEREFORE DO NOT BE FOOLISH, BUT UNDER-
> STAND WHAT THE LORD'S WILL IS."
> (EPHESIANS 5:17)

YOU CAN'T GO WRONG DOING WHAT'S RIGHT

Like Gina, we all wind up in situations that test us. In a matter of seconds we're forced to make a choice that could hurt us or jeopardize our relationships.

If you're a people pleaser—as many girls are, putting acceptance from others over personal well-being and doing anything to stay in someone's good graces (i.e., letting your friend cheat off you so she won't get mad)—you may be scared to risk your relationships. Your friends mean the world to you, so how could you survive without them? What if they dropped you? What if you got left out of parties? What if your best friend chose a new best friend or your boyfriend picked a new girlfriend?

What then?

The root of these what-ifs is fear. And fear doesn't come from God; it comes from the enemy. Satan wants you to believe you'll only be accepted if you follow the crowd. He wants you to believe you have no alternative.

But when it comes to your life, there's *always* a choice. And with God's help and grace, you can face your fears with confidence and choose what's *right* over what seems *safe*. God knows the peer pressure you're up against, and He doesn't leave you alone to deal with it. Throughout Scripture He reminds you not to fear, to leave the future to Him and have faith that He's in control.

Peer pressure isn't something you outgrow. You never reach a point in life where you "figure it all out" and stop feeling tempted. There will always be people who try to persuade you to their way of thinking or make choices for you. It may be new friends or people you love and trust. In some cases, they may think they're doing you a favor. In others, they intentionally hope to mislead you.

Either way, it helps to be prepared. It helps to practice early how to set your limits and say no. Nobody lives a positive life by accident. It takes conscientious effort and deliberation. Deciding ahead of time how you'll handle peer pressure makes you ready when the moment comes.

It's not a matter of *if* you'll be pressured, but *when*.

What you should know is this: *People will push you as far as you let them. Unless you establish parameters now, you'll be talked into things against your better judgment.*

You can't go wrong doing what's right. The safest choice is the right choice because it honors God and allows Him to bless you. I know you want to fit in. I know you want to be popular. But when fitting in and popularity are your goals, you're going to sell out. You'll do things you wouldn't normally do simply to earn approval.

It's okay to be the only person not drinking at a party. It's okay to be the only one not skinny-dipping in the lake. Standing alone may be awkward at first, but people get over it. They quit hounding you once they realize you won't budge. Honestly, you'll be surprised by how much *more* people respect you for not following the crowd. A lot of people wish to be that brave.

As for the friends you fear losing, consider this: Would you drop a friend for making her own choices? If she's into horseback riding and you're into dance, is that a reason to part ways? If she loves Mexican food and you love Italian food, is your friendship doomed?

A true friend wants you to be true to yourself. She respects your choices even if they're different from hers—although she *will* challenge you to grow and reconsider any poor choices you make. The best friends have a lot in common, but they also help fill in each other's voids. Where one is weak, the other is strong.

If someone drops you because you're not playing by their rules, they're not a friend. You don't need their influence. It's a great test to see who stands by, actually, when you're not a puppet. You can weed out the users quickly by seeing who expects you to compromise your values and beliefs.

And since peer approval is fickle, chasing it is like chasing the wind—an impossible quest. Even if you became the most popular girl in school, you'd still be insecure because on any given day, you could lose that popularity. Just one mistake or change in the tide could take you from hero to zero.

Your only security is your relationship with God. Everything else—family, friends, talents, possessions, social status—can change overnight. While the right choice is often the unpopular choice, it's easier to lean that way when you seek affirmation from God, not peers.

Right is right even if nobody is doing it. Wrong is wrong even if everyone is doing it. If standing by your morals distances you from other people sometimes, it's not a sign you're doing it wrong. It's a sign you're doing it *right*.

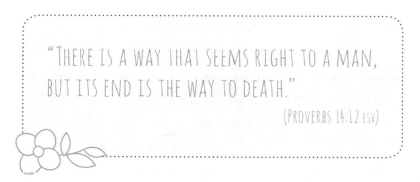

"THERE IS A WAY THAT SEEMS RIGHT TO A MAN, BUT ITS END IS THE WAY TO DEATH."
(PROVERBS 14:12 ESV)

THE GIFT OF YOUR GUT

The first time I tried a cigarette, I was at a restaurant in Dallas with college sorority sisters. Since they all smoked, I decided to try it. Naturally, my friends were happy to show me the ropes.

I wanted to look cool and relaxed like them, but I didn't.

Every time I inhaled, a voice in my head interrupted with thoughts like these:

> *Smoking is bad for me, and I just learned in psychology that nicotine is extremely addictive. Do I really want to get hooked on something I'll have to quit later?*
>
> *Guys say kissing a girl who smokes is like licking an ashtray. Is that what I want my mouth to be, an ashtray?*
>
> *I won't be able to exercise as well if I smoke. The chain smokers I know can barely run a mile. Is it worth it?*
>
> *Smoking will turn my teeth yellow. Gross.*
>
> *I look dumb doing this, plus it tastes disgusting. What's the point?*

In short, I couldn't enjoy that cigarette because my mind rambled. It simply wouldn't stop. It stayed on my case until I heard what I already knew: smoking is a terrible habit that harms the body, and to knowingly do that to myself was foolish.

Like me, you have a conscience. You have gut instincts, hunches, intuition, and a sixth sense about what is good for you. You can push these things down and pretend they don't exist, but you can't make them vanish. God uses these channels to speak to you. Through the Holy Spirit, He may nudge you a certain way or hold you back. Either way, the purpose is to protect you.

Ever wondered why you can't rebel and feel good about it for long? Why does your guilty conscience kick in, often subliminally, when you make bad choices? The internal forces keeping you in check are a gift. They help you recognize when you're headed for trouble.

Imagine if no alarms went off when you were tempted to sin. What would stop you from making one bad choice after another? How would you not harm yourself or others? How could anyone hit rock bottom and decide, "Enough. I'm tired of this lifestyle" if bad decisions brought peace and happiness?

I'll be honest—sometimes I'm annoyed by my conscience and gut feelings. They spoil the fun I want to have. Whether I'm gossiping, overspending, or taking out anger on someone, there are times I want to indulge my will without that voice whispering, "You know this is wrong, Kari. Stop while you're ahead."

Can't a girl sin in peace? Can't I get it out of my system without feeling ashamed or regretful afterward?

The answer is *No*. Sin doesn't work like that—and that's a good thing. You and I both have an innate sense of what's right and wrong. Even if "right" isn't immediately obvious, we know when we're in over our head. Our sins separate us from God, and the only way to close that gap is to admit our sins and ask for forgiveness.

Whether you make good choices or bad ones, you'll sometimes feel uncomfortable. Discomfort is an unavoidable part of the human experience. It's okay to feel uncomfortable because it means you're holding on to what you believe. *If you never felt uncomfortable, you'd never grow and become a better person.*

Whatever your choices are, there will be a trade-off. When you live for your friends, constantly caving to peer pressure, your life will lack inner harmony. You may seem fine on the surface, but deep down there will be an uneasiness you can't shake.

When you live for God, you can enjoy inner harmony but will sometimes feel left out, torn, or lonely when everyone but you jumps on a bandwagon. In times like these, when you're sad because your choices have separated you from friends, ask Jesus to fill the void. Let your relationship with Him help you push through the circumstances.

This world can't offer perfect peace, but there *is* peace in knowing God loves you and has your back. Decide now which comfort you seek: the comfort of fitting in (temporary) or the comfort of pleasing Him (eternal). Get comfortable with being uncomfortable as you tune in to what God tells you. And if you're not sure about something, don't do it.

> "AM I NOW TRYING TO WIN THE APPROVAL OF HUMAN BEINGS, OR OF GOD? OR AM I TRYING TO PLEASE PEOPLE? IF I WERE STILL TRYING TO PLEASE PEOPLE, I WOULD NOT BE A SERVANT OF CHRIST."
>
> (GALATIANS 1:10)

Trusting God helps you trust yourself. It gives you a lead to follow. Many of your friends want to act on their God nudges too. Why not be the one who makes that okay? Why not be the one who makes living in faith an acceptable alternative?

Five Ways to Cope with Peer Pressure

* *Choose the right friends.* Every group has its own culture—a common way of thinking, acting, and behaving. For better or worse, you rub off on each other.

  I mentioned earlier how hanging around a wild crowd impacts your choices. You won't lift them up to higher standards; they'll drag you down to theirs.

  When I was in high school and college, I noticed a phenomenon I still see today: A sweet and innocent girl starts mingling with the wrong crowd by dating the wrong guy. Like Gina from my story, she feels unworthy to be with someone older and more popular.

  What starts as drinks here and there may eventually lead to bigger things, like drug use or sleeping around. This can happen to anyone, not just girls with a wild side. When you consistently expose yourself to negative influences, your resistance weakens.

The right friends won't like you dating the wrong guy. They won't care if he's cool; they'll care about whether you're in safe hands. The right friends can have fun with you anywhere— hanging out in your bedroom, singing in the car, even babysitting your baby sister. They're loyal, loving, and kind.

Most of all, the right friends lift you up. They want you to go places, not fall into ruts.

- *Keep the right attitude.* When you make good choices, stand firm. You don't have to apologize or justify yourself. Be careful, however, not to adopt a false sense of superiority. No one sinner is better than another (Luke 6:41–42). Taking pride in your moral record is a sin in itself.

God calls you to love others, not judge them. People can respect you for being an individual, but when you're self-righteous about it, you're likely to get ostracized. Your peers may also seem particularly *happy* when you make a mistake. We all mess up, and we all need more compassion, not judgment, from others.

- *Choose the right environments.* When it comes down to it, *where you go* matters as much as *who you go with.* Avoid situations that may cause you to slip.

  If you think there will be alcohol or drugs at a party, for instance, skip it. You and your friends can have fun anywhere, so find better things to do, like going to concerts, riding roller coasters, or having a girls' karaoke night.

  Sometimes you'll wind up in a compromising situation by accident. You'll arrive at a party and realize it's *not* the party for you.

  At one social event I went to in college, I heard about some girls and guys snorting cocaine in a bedroom. Since this fraternity was known for drug use, I should have expected this, but I didn't. Fortunately, it was easy to escape. My friends and I said good-bye and left. No harm done.

  But sometimes your escape won't be easy. You may get stuck and need a back-up plan. If you haven't discussed this already, talk to your parents about a "help first, ask questions later" emergency call system. If ever you're in a bind, you can call them for help. They'll pick you up immediately and save the questions for later.

- *Imagine hard scenarios—then imagine a response.* It's tough to think clearly when you're on the spot, especially if you're with someone who makes a bad idea sound good. By thinking ahead about potential tests, you'll be prepared to stand strong.

  How would you handle the following?

  - Your chemistry class has a cheat sheet for today's pop quiz. Everyone has a copy and is memorizing it. You're teetering between a B and a C and need a high score. Do you cheat too?
  - You're at a sleepover where the girls are texting boys. One boy asks a girl to text a picture of her boobs. When she does, the other girls text pictures too. They think it's funny and no big deal. Since you're the only girl holding back, they tease you about being a prude. The guys place bets on you, and one offers three hundred dollars for your prize picture. Do you accept?

- You and your best friends all have a pact: no drinking before age twenty-one and no sex before marriage. But a few weeks ago, while spending the night at one friend's house, she confided to you that she and her boyfriend just went all the way. Now you're at a party, and you see *another* friend accepting a wine cooler. Do you stick to the pact or give in like your friends? Do you say anything to your friends to get them back on track?

- Your boyfriend dumped you for a mean girl. Everyone hates her, and your friends have started a social media smear campaign. They're making up rumors that put a pit in your stomach. Do you let the campaign continue, or do you call it off?

- *Know yourself.* Everyone has weak points and temptation areas. My weakness may not be your weakness, and vice versa. *Whatever is important to you—popularity, money, academic success, pleasing others, perfection—is where* you're most likely to compromise your values. Be honest as you consider your goals and how far you'll go to accomplish them.

"NO TEMPTATION HAS OVERTAKEN YOU EXCEPT WHAT IS COMMON TO MANKIND. AND GOD IS FAITHFUL; HE WILL NOT LET YOU BE TEMPTED BEYOND WHAT YOU CAN BEAR. BUT WHEN YOU ARE TEMPTED, HE WILL ALSO PROVIDE A WAY OUT SO THAT YOU CAN ENDURE IT."

(1 CORINTHIANS 10:13)

SETTING YOURSELF UP TO WIN

There is always a choice with sin. You can engage in it or run from it.

God promises you won't be tempted beyond what you can bear (1 Corinthians 10:13). Whatever the potential sin is, He'll provide a way out. Remember this when you hit a crossroad. Ask for strength and wisdom to handle any situation that tests your resolve.

Keep in mind, too, how resisting temptation makes you stronger and prepares you to handle life's bumpy ride. As the saying goes, "A calm sea never made a good sailor." To grow in faith, you must be willing to endure rough waves.

You'll always have peer pressure in your life. It will take many forms: pressure to rebel, pressure to succeed, pressure to look perfect, pressure to find a great job, pressure to get married, pressure to make money, pressure to buy a big home, pressure to have babies, pressure to raise perfect babies—honestly, it never stops.

Only you can say, "Enough, this is *my life*." Only you can draw boundaries and set yourself up to win by (1) putting faith first, (2) surrounding yourself with positive influences, and (3) expecting to stand alone at times. Accept this now and it won't be a big deal. Mentally, you're prepared.

Feeling uncomfortable is a feeling to trust, not fear. So lean into the awkwardness and ask yourself what lessons you can take away. Weigh the *inner harmony* of living God's way versus the *outer harmony* of living the world's way. Remember that when you choose well, it's easier to love yourself.

Trusting your instincts sharpens your instincts. The sharper they get, the more clearly you see God's presence and understand His will.

DISCUSSION QUESTIONS

1. Do you ever make poor choices to fit in? Does giving in once make it easier to give in again?

2. Do you push friends against their will? Do you lead your friends to get in trouble with you? If so, what does God think of that? What sin do you consider worse, *making* a poor choice or *leading others* to make a poor choice with you?

3. What causes you to stumble? Are there certain people you can't say no to or situations that heighten your insecurities? If so, devise a plan to handle them. Imagine yourself making conscientious choices instead of impulsive ones.

4. On a scale of one to ten, how comfortable are you with being uncomfortable? Do your trust or fear those feelings of discomfort?

5. Why does resisting peer pressure build character? How might a disciplined social life lead to a more disciplined spiritual life?

Chapter 8

Image

Okay, my friend, it's time to talk about your body and how you dress it. I realize this may be slightly embarrassing, but it's important to address the topic.

Upfront you should know three things about your body:

- *Your body is good.*
- *Your body is holy.*
- *Your body holds power.*

If you haven't realized your body's power yet, you will. In the coming years, you'll see how your body can make a boy stop what he's doing and watch you. When this happens, it can feel good. It may make you happy. It may flip on a switch inside that says what you long to hear: *You are pretty. You stand out. You're desirable to the opposite sex.*

What you may also notice is how the fashion choices you make can draw attention from boys. Girls often get misguided here, assuming that all attention is equal. It's not. You see, there is *negative attention* and *positive attention*. While one type hurts you, the other builds you up.

You know the class clown who always interrupts the teacher and thinks he's so funny? That's negative attention. He has an audience, but do they respect him? No, because he's generally rude and annoying. Meanwhile you have the smartest girl in school listening quietly. The room falls silent when she speaks because everyone wonders what she'll say. Is she respected? Yes. And since she doesn't artificially draw the spotlight, the attention she gets is positive.

This same principle applies to clothing. Girls who wear sexy, revealing outfits that make boys do double takes—are they attracting positive attention? Does flashing their skin earn them respect? So many girls interpret this male reaction as a good thing. They think it gives them an upper hand, when really it puts them in a bad position, often leading people to mistakenly devalue them and disregard their true worth.

Using your body to bait boys doesn't enhance their impression of you; it diminishes it. It positions you as a sex symbol in their mind—someone to lust after and use, not love and cherish.

I'm not saying this is right. I'm not excusing any poor behavior or choices boys may make when their sexual instincts get the best of them. *It is every male's responsibility to control his thoughts and desires. Even when a girl dresses sexy, even when a girl misbehaves, she deserves to be treated with respect.*

But what a girl *deserves* and what a girl *gets* don't always mesh. One reason is that we live in an imperfect world. Another reason is that many boys choose to act as predators instead of protectors. They see girls as sexual opportunities. The less clothing a girl wears, the more predators she tends to attract, the bottom of the barrel in terms of recognizing her inherent dignity.

Again, I'm not saying this is right. I'm saying this is reality, a reality of which I want you to be aware.

What you should know is this: *the male brain is wired differently than yours.* While you may feel pretty wearing a short skirt that shows off your legs or a skimpy top that accentuates your tan, boys view this clothing through a different lens.

You see, boys don't admire you the way you admire yourself. While you may simply think you look pretty or fashionable, their mind takes it a step further with questions like, "Wow! I wonder what underwear she's wearing? What does she look like naked? What would she look like naked with *me*?"

That's right, those tiny clothes you may choose to flaunt your figure can actually trigger sexual fantasies in the males around you. The reason they stare is because you're the star of a movie playing in their head. In the book *For Young Women Only*, authors Shaunti Feldhahn and Lisa Rice reveal these insights into the male brain based on interviews with young men.[6] This book is a gem, and I highly recommend it to you.

Here is other food for thought: it isn't just guys your age who may be affected when you flaunt your body. It could be a forty-year-old man—even a sixty-year-old man—who sees you at a football game and suddenly notices you in a new light.

It could be him imagining you naked.

I know, that's disgusting, right? It makes you reconsider what you put on your body.

I know this is uncomfortable to hear, but it's important you understand that these sexual fantasies are common. For a large majority of men, visual temptation is an ongoing struggle. Once a sexual image of you pops into a guy's head, it is stored there. It can come out of his mental file anytime, often involuntarily.

Let's say it together now . . . *ewwwwwwwwwwwwwwwwww.*

Let me throw out that as a teen, I loved miniskirts. I wore them a lot, and my dad didn't like them. I can recall a few times that he told me my skirt was too short and then scowled at it in a way that made me embarrassed. I thought I'd done something wrong, and part of me was angry. I almost wanted to wear my skirt *shorter* just to prove I could.

What I didn't realize was what his scowl meant. It wasn't

me he was thinking about; it was the *reaction* he imagined my skirt might elicit from boys—or even men. That was his fatherly instinct kicking in. He was looking out for his little girl, not wanting anyone to view me as less than I was.

If you, too, have a protective daddy, maybe this helps explain why. Maybe you can understand why he gets upset over your wardrobe choices. It's not so much you he distrusts . . . it's those boys.

And here's the irony: *mothers of boys are equally protective.* Having once been teenagers, they know how girls think. So when girls use their feminine wiles to lure their sons and test them where they may be weak, they know the intention. They see through it, and trust me when I say that is *not* the kind of girl they want their sons to date.

"DO YOU NOT KNOW THAT YOUR BODIES ARE TEMPLES OF THE HOLY SPIRIT, WHO IS IN YOU, WHOM YOU HAVE RECEIVED FROM GOD? YOU ARE NOT YOUR OWN; YOU WERE BOUGHT AT A PRICE. THEREFORE HONOR GOD WITH YOUR BODIES."
(1 CORINTHIANS 6:19-20)

RESPECTING YOUR BODY

Now that I've shared reasons to dress appropriately, the questions become: What is a girl to do? Should you swear off shopping? Those great skinny jeans you just saw on sale—are you supposed to look the other way?

Rest assured that you can still have fun with fashion. You can express yourself through clothes and build a stylish wardrobe if you desire. I understand the magic of the right outfit, and I'm not about to take that away from you. After all, taking on the world is easier when you feel you're dressed the part, right?

Just remember your body was made to be celebrated, not flaunted. Your clothes should reflect who you are inside. As a child of God, loved beyond your imagination, you want people to notice your total package—not how much skin you're showing, or how tight your dress is.

Early in this chapter, I gave you three important facts about your body. Two of them override everything you'll hear. No matter who you are, what mistakes you may have made, or how others view you, you can cling to these truths:

- *Your body is good.*
- *Your body is holy.*

Yes, your body has the potential to make men lust. Yes, it can trigger sexual fantasies you have absolutely nothing to do with.

Does this mean your body is bad or something to be ashamed of? NO!

Your body is a miracle. It is a gift. It is the house for an invisible God dwelling inside you through the Holy Spirit. If your friend needs a hug, God can't physically embrace her, but you can. Your body allows you to spread God's love. And when you use your body in beautiful ways, you set your soul in motion. You become a vessel God can work through.

The effect your body may have on a boy is *his battle to fight*. He can't blame you for any urges or fantasy flicks that get stirred. But since boys are your brothers in Christ, you should want to help them. You should have compassion for their struggles just as they should have compassion for yours.

So don't diminish yourself by acting seductive, wearing inappropriate clothes, and throwing yourself on boys. Don't tease them, play games, and make racy comments. This behavior isn't classy, and the strategy will hurt you. When you fail to treat boys like real people, they'll fail to treat you like a real person too.

The battle *you* must fight is the temptation to use your body and inappropriate clothing to get ahead, get noticed, or get what you want. For too many girls, it's an easy shortcut. But what this path of least resistance leads to is dead ends, disappointment, and the wrong kind of admirers.

The way you dress affects how people perceive you and receive you. When you use your body as God intends, you experience the joy that comes full circle when you're treated the way you deserve.

> "FOR EVERYTHING IN THE WORLD—THE LUST OF THE FLESH, THE LUST OF THE EYES, AND THE PRIDE OF LIFE—COMES NOT FROM THE FATHER BUT FROM THE WORLD."
>
> (1 JOHN 2:16)

QUICK QUIZ: Do Your Friends Influence Your Clothes?

You're on a girls' beach trip and everyone is getting ready for dinner. Throughout the condominium, hair dryers are buzzing.

In a small bathroom, you apply makeup, fix your hair, and smile at your reflection in the mirror. You feel good about your look tonight. The long maxi dress accentuates your height and lean physique.

But as you walk in the den, your heart sinks. Suddenly you don't feel good anymore, because compared to the other girls—all dressed sexy in metallic short shorts, wedge sandals, and tight tank tops—your look is unexciting.

What do you do?

A. You rush back into your bedroom and change into the sexiest outfit you can find. Competing with so many beautiful girls is hard enough. How will boys notice you if you don't show off your body too?

B. You don't change clothes, but you don't bounce back either. Already your night is ruined because you feel insecure and overshadowed.

C. You stick with what you have on and remember how pretty you felt when you looked in the mirror. If you had confidence then, shouldn't you have confidence now?

D. You get over it and quit the comparisons. Everybody has their own style, and even if you're the only one dressed modestly, it works for you.

If you answered "C" or "D," you're on the right track. You understand how the answer isn't less clothing but more radiance. The best-dressed girls leave something to the imagination. Dare to be different from the trendsetters who bare it all, and let your beauty speak for itself.

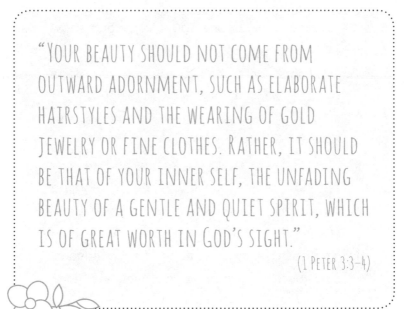

"YOUR BEAUTY SHOULD NOT COME FROM OUTWARD ADORNMENT, SUCH AS ELABORATE HAIRSTYLES AND THE WEARING OF GOLD JEWELRY OR FINE CLOTHES. RATHER, IT SHOULD BE THAT OF YOUR INNER SELF, THE UNFADING BEAUTY OF A GENTLE AND QUIET SPIRIT, WHICH IS OF GREAT WORTH IN GOD'S SIGHT."

(1 PETER 3:3–4)

MATCHING YOUR INTERIOR TO YOUR EXTERIOR

How would you feel if you bit into a Reese's cup . . . and it tasted like vinegar?

What if you rented *Pitch Perfect* . . . but saw *The Smurfs* play on the screen instead?

What if you opened a can of sardines . . . and discovered a diamond inside?

How would you react to these scenarios? Would you feel confused? Shocked? Completely caught off-guard?

The package of a product parallels what clothes do for us: They create expectations. They offer hints of what's in store. They tell our story in three seconds or less.

I'm sure you know the saying "You can't judge a book by its cover." The reality, however, is that people do. People look at your presentation to see if your story warrants a closer look. Just as the cover of this book reflects what I've written, your packaging should reflect your true self.

Not who you *want* to be, but who you *are*.

It sounds simple, but what complicates your mission is the degrading trend in girls' clothing. Let me just say, *you're too good for these trends*. You deserve better than low-cut shirts, microminis, and dresses not long enough to cover your bottom. You deserve better than the messages these clothes send out and the rash assumptions people make as a result.

Now, you may believe a girl should be able to wear anything she wants and not be judged. You may argue that there's nothing wrong in showing cleavage and wearing skirts that skim your panty line when you bend over. It's a free world, and how you dress is your prerogative.

How you dress *is* your prerogative. But when you dress

promiscuously, people will assume you're on board with that lifestyle. Guys—particularly predators—will take it as an invitation to be more aggressive and less cautious. They'll talk to you differently, think about you differently, and treat you differently. They'll handle you like a girl whose package screams "Easy" rather than a girl whose package screams "Respect."

Packaging matters, and if you want people to care more about your story than your body, follow this motto when shopping: more class, less skin.

Dressing with class means keeping it tasteful. It means seeking inspiration from icons like Kate, the Duchess of Cambridge, and not over-the-top rock stars. It means asking certain questions when testing an outfit:

- Does this make me look *beautiful* or *sexy*?
- Does this represent who I am inside? Is it too tight or too short? Does it *reflect* my inherent dignity or *distract* from it?
- Does this complement my body, or does it seek attention?
- What "story" does this outfit tell? Is that the story I want told?
- Would I want my grandfather/youth leader/preacher to see me wearing this? What about my future employer?

I love a girl with her own flair. I love how some girls wear hats and scarves, while others wear headbands. Some girls favor bold, splashy prints, while others stick with earth tones. Some

like to dress funky and fun, while others keep it conservative
and simple.

Style is a personal preference, and there's no one right way.
What makes you feel good and comfortable is something you
decide for yourself.

But whatever your style is, steer clear of the "barely there"
trends. The world's Minimalist Clothing Movement for Girls
is based on this lie: *You need skimpy clothes to compete with
other girls wearing skimpy clothes. Without them, you can't catch
a guy.*

Here is my argument: If you catch a guy because you've
revealed your body, you're starting off on the wrong foot. It
won't be a healthy relationship, and it won't be long before the
novelty of your body wears off and his attention turns to someone else wearing a provocative outfit.

*Your body is no different from the bodies of a thousand other
girls in short skirts.* What it can deliver to a guy, countless other
bodies can deliver too. If your body is the foundation you're
building upon, you're in for trouble. Expect a rocky ride and
lots of insecurity because you've made yourself easy to replace.

If you want to be irreplaceable . . . if you want to shine . . . if
you want to distinguish yourself from other girls . . . focus on
what no one can compete with: your inner authenticity. You are
the only you in the universe; no one comes close to competing
with that. Your interior can't be replicated.

And while guys may not realize this yet, that interior—that
inner mystery—is what they'll always chase. It is more valuable,

distinctive, and interesting than your short-term package, which may look like the package of thirty other girls.

So let your presentation capture your essence. Make the visible reflect the invisible.

Don't be a diamond hiding inside a can of sardines. Be a diamond hiding inside a velvet box, ready to shine in the big reveal.

Your body is good. Your body is holy. Your body holds power. Even if you've made mistakes with your body, it isn't too late to turn it around. Our God is a God of second chances, and He doesn't want anyone to miss out on how incredible you are. Remember, you're His masterpiece, more worthy than all the riches on earth.

Your body was made to glorify God. And when your clothes honor Him, you're dressed to change the world.

DISCUSSION QUESTIONS

1. What do *you* think when you see a girl in revealing clothes? Do you notice her beauty, or does your mind jump to negative conclusions?

2. Has a guy ever made a disrespectful remark about your body? Has anyone checked you out in a way that made you uncomfortable? How can you remember the big truths about your body—that it's good and holy—when someone treats you like a sex object or chooses to act as a predator instead of a protector?

3. How can a girl have fun with fashion and still look classy?

4. Turning the tables, how should guys dress? Does it enhance your impression when they're showered and shaved? Who would you rather have pick you up for a date, a guy dressed sloppily (grungy T-shirt and jeans) or someone pulled together (button-down and khakis)?

5. How can you use your body to glorify God? How can you be a vessel of God's love, power, and grace?

Chapter 9

Inner Beauty

Truth #2: Pretty girls are a dime a dozen. Outer beauty attracts attention, but inner beauty is what holds it.

Amanda couldn't figure out what her problem was. Getting boyfriends was ridiculously easy, but hanging on to them was another story.

Since her sixteenth birthday two years ago, she'd had seven serious relationships. They all followed the same pattern: She'd meet a guy who was crazy about her. They'd date seriously for three or four months. Then out of the blue, he'd back off and say he needed "space."

Amanda hated the word *space*. It made it sound like she was suffocating them, when it was always her boyfriends who came on strong. At least at first they did. And that is what confused Amanda.

Why did they always start off obsessed and attentive, then lose interest once they *knew* her? Was it the commitment that scared them off—or was something wrong with her?

Amanda knew she was beautiful. People complimented her looks all the time—so often, in fact, it got old. Whenever she went to a restaurant or shopping, men would stop and stare, and some of her friends had a problem with that. They said it made them feel invisible, and it was better for their self-esteem if Amanda stayed home.

Those comments hurt, but when you're beautiful, people think they can say anything because you're confident enough to take it. Only Amanda wasn't confident, and that's why she liked hanging around the guys. Unlike females, they didn't tear her down. They didn't get jealous over petty things or try to undermine her.

Lately, however, even boys had disappointed Amanda. Her last boyfriend dumped her for another girl, and the one before him accused her of being boring and vain.

"You're dumb as rocks!" he screamed in their final fight. "Maybe if you spent less time in front of the mirror, you'd get a personality!"

Amanda had thrown a shoe at him, screaming back that *he* was the one who insisted she look hot every time they went out. This boyfriend liked treating Amanda to expensive gifts and fancy dates, and in return he wanted Amanda to "make him look good."

She'd done him a favor, and to insult her for that took a lot of nerve.

Amanda was tired of being used. She'd had enough of investing *everything* in relationships and getting kicked to the curb. Was she dating the wrong guys, or were they all commitment-phobes? Was she foolish to hold out hope that a boy would ever stay?

Something had to change, but what? Amanda couldn't quite figure that out.

> "BUT THE LORD SAID TO SAMUEL, 'DO NOT CONSIDER HIS APPEARANCE OR HIS HEIGHT, FOR I HAVE REJECTED HIM. THE LORD DOES NOT LOOK AT THE THINGS PEOPLE LOOK AT. PEOPLE LOOK AT THE OUTWARD APPEARANCE, BUT THE LORD LOOKS AT THE HEART.'"
>
> (1 SAMUEL 16:7)

WHAT'S BEHIND YOUR STOREFRONT WINDOW?

There is no denying that beauty opens doors.

Being pretty gets you noticed. It attracts boys. People are

more likely to smile at you for no reason and listen when you speak. Should you get pulled over for speeding, you might be able to sweet-talk your way out of it. Without a doubt, being pretty has its perks.

But all too often with girls, appearance becomes overly valued and too important. You can channel so much time and energy into your looks you neglect the hidden parts of you that possess *more* value, like your personality, talent, smarts, sense of humor, and spiritual life.

What results is a dazzling shell that's hollow inside. While the package may look attractive, there is very little substance below the surface.

What you should know is this: *Being pretty isn't enough. Being hot isn't enough. Being flawless and physically perfect isn't enough.* Pretty girls are a dime a dozen, and unless you have other things in your favor, you won't stand out for long.

In Amanda's story, the root problem was her overreliance on her looks. Since that is what people marveled over, she mistakenly believed it was her best asset and focused hard on it. Like many beautiful girls, Amanda "put it all in the storefront window." She was all about the display and presentation.

But think about the storefront windows you see while shopping. When you run across one that is spectacular, aren't you especially excited to see what's inside? Don't you hope the interior matches the exterior—or better yet, surpasses it?

And when you walk in and discover a dull interior, how do you feel? Disappointed? Letdown? Antsy to move on? Maybe the store is boring. Maybe there's dead space. Maybe the environment is cold and intimidating—not the kind of place you want to hang out.

Whatever the case, it is not enough that the storefront window catches your eye from the street. How comfortable you feel *inside* the store is what keeps you coming back.

People are the same way. Your appearance is a starting point, an invitation for others to look closer. The most beautiful people have interiors that outshine their exteriors, exceeding anyone's expectations.

They are first and foremost beautiful souls.

Let's be clear: appearance is important. To boldly serve God, you need to be happy with how you look, and that begins with taking care of the one body you've been given. When you are put together, people can take you seriously. They're more willing to follow you, take a chance on you, and help you reach your dreams.

But there comes a point where enough is enough. Looking good could be a full-time job, and for some girls it is.

When this becomes your lifestyle choice, however, you fail to cultivate the rich interior life you need to find true happiness and intimacy with God. You attract friends and guys who are equally caught up in appearances, which makes for shallow and flimsy relationships.

That was Amanda's other problem: the boys she drew weren't the type to appreciate a girl's depth and authenticity; they were boys who chase anything that makes their eyes pop out. You can't count on these guys because there will always be another store-front window that comes along and outshines yours.

Being pretty, hot, or physically perfect isn't enough. And when your display is your obsession, the mystery behind the curtain gets neglected or, worse yet, forgotten.

> "CHARM IS DECEPTIVE, AND BEAUTY IS FLEETING; BUT A WOMAN WHO FEARS THE LORD IS TO BE PRAISED."
> (PROVERBS 31:30)

HOW YOU ACT IMPACTS HOW PEOPLE SEE YOU

When I started college, I got a crash course on beauty that changed my lens forever.

From day one on campus at the University of Alabama, I was blown away by all the gorgeous girls. Everywhere I looked there were knock-outs, girls to suit any taste or preference: tall, short, curvy, lean, blonde, brunette, glamorous, natural—you get the idea.

It was an intimidating set-up, especially when I considered how freshman girls outnumbered freshman boys. As I thought about the dates I hoped to have and calculated the odds stacked against me, I wondered how I was supposed to compete.

During the next four years, I found out. Above all, I learned that beauty is a running tally influenced by a girl's choices. You see, *how a girl acts impacts how people see her.*

When you show love, like comforting a friend during a break-up, you become more attractive. Your beauty quotient rises. But when you act selfishly, choosing instead to *pursue* your friend's ex-boyfriend, your beauty quotient drops.

It really is that simple.

A lot of outwardly beautiful girls make themselves ugly by acting catty, vindictive, or promiscuous. They start as a ten and fall to a seven on the beauty scale as their true colors show. Then there are girls with so much character and inner light that they transform from a seven into a ten. Once you know them, a deeper beauty shines through.

This deeper beauty is God's presence. When you reveal your godliness to others, they notice it and *feel* it. They crave your company and see you through new, enlightened eyes.

This is why an eighty-year-old grandmother can be the most beautiful creature on earth to her grandchild. It's why you may suddenly be attracted to a guy you never found attractive before, because one life-changing conversation stirred up something wonderful and miraculous inside you.

There are two types of beauty: beauty in the eye and beauty in the mind. While the eye's opinion matters initially when a first impression is made, the mind's opinion stands the test of time.

The better you know someone, the less their appearance

matters. Even their most arresting features don't grab you like before.

The best part of you—or anyone else—isn't readily apparent. Even if you won the genetic lottery and look like a supermodel, this holds true. While the world pushes physical perfection, pressuring you to chase the eye's approval, God looks deeper.

God's primary concern is not your body, which will expire one day, but your soul, which lives forever.

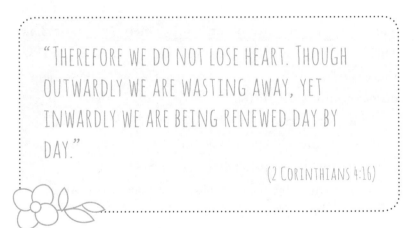

"THEREFORE WE DO NOT LOSE HEART. THOUGH OUTWARDLY WE ARE WASTING AWAY, YET INWARDLY WE ARE BEING RENEWED DAY BY DAY."

(2 CORINTHIANS 4:16)

THE BEAUTY OF LOVING YOURSELF

I've discussed vanity, but for most girls, the big issue with beauty is insecurity.

In some way, we all doubt God's handiwork. We question the way He built us. We admire other women and wish we looked like them. If we're short, we wish we were tall. If our hair is curly, we wish it was straight. If we're brunette, we wish we were blonde. If we're big-boned, we wish we were thin.

The wish list never ends, does it?

Then there's that bully in our head, the ruthless inner critic who seeks to destroy. I don't know about yours, but mine is sharp and mean. He knows my weak points and how to target them. Where I'm sensitive and easily hurt, that's where he strikes. I have to stay on guard against my bully and know when he's attacking me, because otherwise he'll cut straight to my heart.

Your inner critic can cause tremendous harm, and it's important you understand this. Since he's aware of vulnerabilities you'd never admit to anyone, he can go for the kill. All criticism hurts, but that voice between your ears can absolutely destroy you. Whether you believe or dismiss his lies brings death or life into your soul.

As I mentioned earlier, that unforgiving voice in your head isn't the voice of God; it's the voice of the devil. God would never speak to you with such harsh, unkind, and unloving words. So instead of handing your inner bully a megaphone, make a point to muzzle him. Remember that *you* control *him*, and the reason he'll pull any stop to beat you down is because he doesn't want you to serve God.

By turning you against yourself, he messes with your confidence. He keeps you from seeing yourself in a favorable light so you'll want to retreat into your shell and hide instead of stepping out in faith to change the world.

So how do you conquer your inner bully? How do you turn

self-doubt into self-love? How do you embrace yourself and find confidence even as you work through an issue that has you down—like trying to reach a healthy weight, treating your acne, or growing out a tragic haircut?

This is how: *By showing yourself grace. By seeing yourself through God's loving, merciful eyes.* Remember, you are His child. He made you in His image and is PROUD of the result. God loves you equally at your best and your worst, and with His help you can replace the negativity in your head with hope, love, and truth. His love endures forever (Psalm 136).

When you look in the mirror, find reasons to praise God. Let your eyes magnify what's right and minimize what's wrong. Take captive every thought you have, and make it obedient to Christ (2 Corinthians 10:5).

- Instead of criticizing your heavy thighs . . . praise God for two legs that let you run, dance, swim, and climb.
- Instead of wishing your eyes were blue . . . praise Him because you can see.
- Instead of crying because you're too tall . . . praise Him for your speed and agility.
- Instead of picking your body apart . . . praise Him for how the parts function together, allowing you to impact lives.

Your mind is going to chatter. It will speak love, hate, and everything in between. The thoughts you entertain form a track on which your self-esteem runs. While godly thoughts create a

loop of confidence, self-destructive ones create a cycle of insecurity that's hard to break.

Decide now to love yourself through God's eyes. Silence
your inner bully by keeping his motive in mind. Ask yourself
if you'd ever speak to a friend the way you speak to yourself. If
the answer is no, take it as a sign to change your self-talk.

There is beauty in all God's creation, and that creation
includes *you*. By recognizing yourself as His masterpiece, made
by the same hands that created the oceans, the sun, and every
bird in the sky, you can see yourself through the proper lens,
one that evokes awe toward Him.

"THOSE WHO LOOK TO HIM ARE RADIANT; THEIR
FACES ARE NEVER COVERED WITH SHAME."
(PSALM 34:5)

Quick Quiz: Does Your Appearance Rule Your Social Life?

For months you've counted down the days
until your friend's birthday bash. Her parents
have planned a lavish celebration with a band,
fireworks, and three hundred guests.

The day of the party, however, you don't want to go. First of all, you look terrible in your new dress because your stomach is bloated from that time of the month. Second, your eyes are puffy from crying after a fight with your mom. Third, you woke up this morning with a zit the size of Texas on your chin.

What do you do?

A. You skip the party. After all, you can't go out in public in this condition. People will talk! You'd be a drag anyway, and that's unfair to your friend. With all those guests there, she won't notice your absence.

B. You find another dress to wear, fix your eyes with makeup, and go to the party. Even though you don't feel like being social, you make yourself have fun. This is your friend, after all, and it's only right to support her.

C. You wear sunglasses to the party, sulk in the corner, and spend the night thinking about how your friend owes you for this sacrifice you've made.

D. You look in the mirror and tell yourself what

you need to hear: "Snap out of it! Tonight isn't about you. It's about the birthday girl!"

If you answered "B" or "D," you're thinking correctly. You've put your friend over a bad hair day and the bad attitude that can result. All of us have days we don't want to leave the house, but sometimes we have to. Sometimes we have to get over our issues and insecurities to show up for the people we love.

A friend's birthday party is always a special event. Even if three hundred guests come, your friend will notice—and remember—who is and isn't there.

WHAT'S A HEALTHY SELF-IMAGE?

A girl I know got liposuction at age nineteen because her mom insisted. Her mom wanted her to be a beauty queen, and since this girl was naïve, she went along with it.

Her mom isn't a terrible person, and in many ways she's a loving parent. But what this shows is how the pressure to look perfect and fit a mold can come from anyone—even those closest to you.

That is why *you* need to understand what a healthy self image is. You can't rely on the world's opinion because humans get it wrong sometimes. Only God is completely accurate. Only God can tell you the truth, and nothing but the truth, about your beauty.

When I was your age, I loved *Teen* magazine. *Teen* is where I learned about fashion, boys, and makeup because the Internet didn't exist. As much as I loved flicking through the magazine, however, it always triggered some deep insecurities. The images made me feel less than, inadequate, and not enough.

After all, the models were flawless. Compared to them, I felt pitiful. I can't tell you how many hours I spent staring at their pictures, trying to figure out what their secrets were so I could achieve their level of beauty.

My thoughts sounded like this:

Her eyes are perfectly symmetrical. How do I get my eyes like that?

How do I make my thin hair thick like hers?

I wish my legs were that skinny!

I'd kill for her stomach!

Even her toes are perfect!

Suffice it to say, my model study sessions never ended well. They brought me down and discouraged me because I wanted to look *exactly* like them and *nothing* like me.

Fortunately, my *Teen* magazine came only once a month. That gave me a break from the models, a stretch of several weeks where I could forget about the gap between their beauty and mine.

But you? You live in a different time. You're reminded of that gap *every day*. In addition to airbrushed photos of movie stars on the Internet, you see filtered pictures of your friends and peers all over social media. Every time you scroll down, you see someone putting their best foot forward, showing the one picture out of twenty attempts that captured a perfect moment.

And when you see these perfect moments, you assume other girls have perfect lives. You wonder what their secrets are, because judging by appearances, they have the answers.

But guess what? They don't. Just like you, every girl out there is searching. She's measuring herself against someone she thinks is *prettier*, *happier*, or *better off* than she is. She's studying pictures to see who has all the answers. She's feeling less than, inadequate, and not enough.

Do you see the cycle? Do you see why girls become jealous, insecure, and competitive? When you think someone has the secrets you want, you tend to resent them. That resentment builds walls instead of bridges and turns girls into threats instead of allies.

A healthy self-image starts with love and compassion—for yourself *and* others. It looks for common ground. Beneath our appearances, we all share the same emotions:

- Joy and sadness
- Hope and fear
- Gratitude and anger
- Courage and self-doubt
- Empathy and indifference
- Certainty and confusion

Every girl you know is in the same boat as you. You all face pressures to look perfect. You all share an unspoken understanding of how hard it is growing up. And when you focus on your common core, you quit feeling threatened. You see yourselves as allies and stop the constant comparisons.

Once the comparisons stop, real progress begins. You no longer feel superior to some girls and inferior to others. God created you with great intention and attention. No detail is a mistake because God doesn't make mistakes. While there will always be parts of your appearance you wish to change, it's what you *do with those wishes* that affects your self-esteem.

If you fixate on the traits you want to change, jumping on the "wish" train every time it passes ("I wish I had a fast metabolism," "I wish I had her nose"), you'll live with an anxious, dissatisfied heart. You'll fool yourself into believing that one day you'll arrive at your destination, a place where you can accept what you see *at last* because your flaws have been perfected.

This destination doesn't exist, of course, and that is why this mind-set is unhealthy. When you chase perfection, there is no end in sight, no place to get off, no reprieve for your anxious heart.

But if you let Jesus fill your gap, that void between where you are and where you wish to be, you find peace *exactly* where you are. You don't jump on every "wish" train or live for the day you'll finally accept yourself, because you accept yourself *now*—even if there's room to improve, even if you're working toward positive changes, even if you don't fit beauty stereotypes. The heart of a healthy self-image is self-love, and the heart of self-love is God.

When you feel less than, inadequate, and not enough, you're thinking with the mind of the world. Think instead with the mind of God. Define beauty as *variety* and marvel over God's genius, revealed by His making no two people the same.

You were made to be perfectly you—and no one else. While the world wants to box you in, imposing standards and expectations, God will set you free. His concern is to get you heaven-ready, not magazine-ready, and as you embrace this reality, you form a healthy self-image that's based on truth, love, and God's abundant grace.

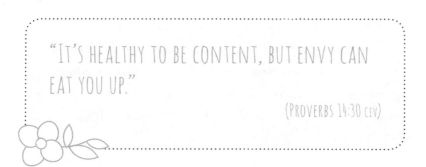

"IT'S HEALTHY TO BE CONTENT, BUT ENVY CAN EAT YOU UP."

(PROVERBS 14:30 CEV)

FALLING IN LOVE WITH YOUR SOUL

Life is so very short. Even if you live ninety years, that's a blip compared to the infinite time you'll spend in eternity.

When you die, your outer beauty dies with you. It's buried six feet under. At your funeral, people won't be talking about your sculpted abs, your bleached teeth, or your lush eyelashes (at least I hope not). They'll talk about what kind of person you were and how you touched their lives.

So ask yourself, "What do I want said at my funeral? What value am I adding to the lives around me?" Does your outer beauty make anyone a better person? Does it feed someone's soul the way a soul longs to be fed?

How you make others feel *inside* is what sets you apart from other girls. That is what makes you the girl a guy can't live without. While physical attraction is important, it isn't the force that will make your husband-to-be imagine a *future* together, a lifelong journey filled with children, grandchildren, and great-grandchildren.

The most beautiful girls inspire others and lift them up. They are first and foremost beautiful souls. Since it's the quality of your soul, not your flesh, that determines where you spend eternity, pay attention to it. Tend to your soul with the same care you give your body. Treat it as something sacred, because it is.

After all, your soul is your ticket to heaven. And since you only get one, it is paramount to nurture it wisely.

DISCUSSION QUESTIONS

1. Why does obsessing over appearance set girls up for disappointment?

2. When you see a girl who's prettier than you, do you automatically dislike her? Could you be friends with her, or would that trigger too much insecurity?

3. What does your inner critic tell you? How can you replace his lies with God's truth?

4. Is physical perfection your goal? If so, how does the quest affect your self-esteem and self-worth?

5. What does a beautiful soul look like? Who in your life possesses an inner beauty that makes them radiant?

Chapter 10

Self-Talk

> Truth #1: The source of all peace and happiness lives inside you. Learn to listen to the whispers of God over the megaphone of public opinion.

I couldn't find my cell phone anywhere.

I'd called it twenty times and searched every room of my parents' beach home. I knew it was nearby, yet no matter how hard I listened, I couldn't hear a *hint* of a ring.

Frustrated and fed up, I stopped in the kitchen and tried to think. *If I were a cell phone, where would I be? Did I accidentally throw it away like I've done before?* I checked the trash can, but it wasn't there. I'd exhausted all my options. I didn't know what to try next.

Then suddenly it hit me—maybe if I got the house really

quiet, I could hear better. Because the air conditioner was creating a low hum, I turned it off. Immediately the house grew still. I knew I was on the right track.

I called my phone again, and several seconds later I heard a tiny, faint ring. It was so light and barely perceptible I questioned whether I was imagining it. Oddly enough, the ring seemed to originate below the house, which was built over a carport and storage room. Since I knew my phone wasn't down there, I dismissed the thought.

But after attempting several more calls, I heard that faint ring again coming from below the house. It was an impossible thought because I hadn't been down there all morning. By this point, however, I was desperate enough to try anything.

So I walked out the front door of my parents' beach home, certain this was a waste of time, and called my phone again. This time I didn't have to listen hard because, much to my amazement . . . the ring got louder!

I wasn't crazy after all. My cell phone *was* below the house.

It turned out that I was right about accidentally throwing my phone away in the trash. Someone had then taken that trash bag outside for the collection. Laughing at myself, yet totally grossed out, I dug out my device from a large pile of garbage.

Not my finest moment, but at least I had my phone back.

In many ways, this story illustrates how God works in my life and yours. We want His call to be loud and obvious, but most often it's subtle. We have to turn off all the background noise to catch it. We doubt ourselves and wonder if we're imagining things. We think crazy possibilities then quickly dismiss them. We stay put instead of venturing out because venturing out requires us to leave our comfort zone.

But there comes a point when we're so desperate we'll try anything. We step outside the box to see if that faint call we hear from afar is real. We open our heart and mind, listen once again, and voilá . . . discover the answer is right under our nose.

Our mind wasn't playing tricks after all. At last it's all so clear.

Am I suggesting that God leads us to the trash? No, of course not. I'm saying that God leads us to unexpected places, venues we might never visit by our own volition. And when we keep our heart and mind open to that, trusting our instincts and testing out those far-fetched possibilities, we get a clearer picture of what direction God is nudging us toward.

"HE SAYS, 'BE STILL, AND KNOW THAT I AM GOD; I WILL BE EXALTED AMONG THE NATIONS, I WILL BE EXALTED IN THE EARTH.'"

(PSALM 46:10)

YOUR GOD-SHAPED HOLE

It started innocently enough, with a fantastic lavender dress I bought to wear on Easter.

I wanted my daughters to wear white dresses, and since my oldest had recently experienced a growth spurt, we ran around town searching for a white dress we agreed on. Reaching a compromise was painful. There were eye rolls, scowls, and tears inside many dressing rooms. I'm sure you can relate.

At last we found a dress—but then we needed shoes for her and her sister. I also needed makeup and a host of other things to help our family look nice and presentable on Easter morning.

What started as a simple effort became a scavenger hunt as I traveled from store . . . to store . . . to store to assemble my family's wardrobe.

It was the middle of Holy Week when I was able to step outside myself and watch this frantic woman struggle to pull it together. Only then did I realize how I'd *completely* strayed from the whole point of Easter. Here I was, preparing for the biggest spiritual day of the year, and the overriding emotion inside me was emptiness and a lack of purpose. It wasn't Jesus' fault by any means, because this was *all me.*

Instead of using the Easter season to fill up on Christ, staring at the cross and reflecting, I'd been staring at shopping racks. I'd let material pursuits distract me, and as a result I felt deeply dissatisfied.

What you should know is this: *inside all of us is a God-shaped hole that only God can fill.* He created us for eternity, and that spiritual space represents our innate desire to connect with Him.

But when we try stuffing earthly pleasures into that space— clothes, money, relationships, success—we grow unhappy. We create a black hole of desire that can't be quenched because we're filling up on empty calories. The more we have, the more we need.

My Easter shopping mission was a misguided attempt to fill my God-shaped hole. I substituted my family's outward presentation at church for spiritual growth, and the fit was completely off, like forcing a square peg into a round hole.

Sometimes, however, what I stuff into my God-shaped hole works like putty. It fills the gap temporarily. I'll think I'm complete until suddenly, without warning, the void reopens, emptying me out again.

Think for a moment about your life. What earthly pleasures do you stuff in your God-shaped hole? What distractions get you off track and lead you down dead-end roads?

God calls you to live a simple life. He knows that less is more. Once your basic needs for food, shelter, and clothing are met, you shouldn't need much. Those things alone *should* sustain you. But do they? No. Why? Because the world we live in likes to complicates things.

According to the world, the basics are never enough. More is never enough. To be content is to settle . . . and to settle is to get left behind.

Why buy a twenty-dollar shirt when there are shirts for a hundred dollars? Why eat pasta when there is lobster? Why own *one* pair of designer jeans when you can own a *dozen* like the best-dressed girls in school?

Listening to what the world defines as important—fame, fortune, power, notoriety—creates unrest inside you. It sends you on wild goose chases for temporal things you think will satisfy your need for *more.*

But the craving that never leaves you isn't a craving for more stuff. It's a craving for more God. He designed you to seek Him. He gave you a heart for heaven to help draw you home. Even your best moments on earth can't compare to the joy that awaits you and me in our final resting place.

To tune out the world, tune into God's voice. Cut back the noise, chaos, and busyness of your life that buffers you from Him. Remember how I had to make my parents' beach home really quiet to hear the call? Your life works the same way. When you eliminate the distractions, you start to notice your faint call from God.

God will tell you where to walk next. He'll come to you wherever you are and show you the next right move. But He won't reveal His master plan at once. Your spiritual journey is step-by-step. It requires faith, trust, and complete reliance on the One who loves you most.

So if you don't have your whole life planned out, don't worry. God has it covered. He may call you into unfamiliar territory, but with Jesus by your side to help you, you can handle it.

What God wants from you is obedience. Once you turn down the volume of external chatter, you allow His voice to break through and speak words of hope, joy, and life.

> "MANY ARE THE PLANS IN A PERSON'S HEART, BUT IT IS THE LORD'S PURPOSE THAT PREVAILS."
> (PROVERBS 19:21)

ARE YOU READY TO SURRENDER?

It took me forty years to truly understand what surrendering to God means.

I pray you'll be smarter than I was. I hope you'll understand early why surrendering to Him isn't a defeat. It's a VICTORY.

In the Lord's prayer we say, "Thy (God's) will be done." But do we embrace that in real life? Do we put God's will over our will? Not always. You see, we humans are selfish. We tend to be control freaks. We hate being told what to do. We're like those stubborn kids who run off from their parents at the mall because their parents won't let them eat cotton candy and Skittles for lunch.

And what happens after they're separated from their parents? They start to get lonely and scared, right? They look around and realize the world is bigger and more confusing than they thought. Suddenly lost and unsure, they regret their rash decision. They wish they had someone who had their back again, a strong and capable adult.

Life is hard, and when you try going about it alone, it will soon become impossible.

I've tried running away from God. I've gotten mad because a prayer wasn't answered the way I wanted or because He allowed something bad to happen. But what I've discovered is that distancing myself from God only hurts me. It deepens the gulf of loneliness and fear.

My big surrender to God came late in life and by necessity, not choice. It happened during a very stressful period where I begged for help daily because I couldn't handle my life alone. I was tired of trying, tired of being tough, tired of trying to stay strong when what I *really* wanted to do was fall to my knees.

As I admitted my weaknesses—not in a single day, but over several months—a massive burden lifted off my shoulders. My heart began to change, and the old dreams I had, inspired by the world, transformed into new dreams inspired by God. I was happier and felt more like myself, even though my new focus was less about me and more about God.

Surrendering to God isn't a one-time event. It's a daily choice. Some days you'll get it right, and other days you won't. But even if you don't, even if you run away, God accepts you and welcomes you back. His love and grace are perpetual, available without conditions or limits.

Are you ready to be a vessel for God? Can you say, "Use me, Lord?" Can you chase big dreams with all your heart, yet accept any outcome in God's will? Do you understand your surrender as a triumph because it allows God to work through you in powerful ways?

If you've answered yes, you're ready to surrender. You're ready to show the world what you've got.

Now the question is, "Is the world ready for you?"

> "IF WE CONFESS OUR SINS, HE IS FAITHFUL AND JUST AND WILL FORGIVE US OUR SINS AND PURIFY US FROM ALL UNRIGHTEOUSNESS."
>
> (1 JOHN 1:9)

DISCUSSION QUESTIONS

1. How does God work in your life? When His call is faint, do you pay attention to it or dismiss it?

2. What earthly pleasures get stuffed in your God-shaped hole? Why can't they satisfy you for long?

3. Have you ever run away from God? If so, what happened? Did your life get better when you wrote Him off, or did you wind up feeling too far away from home?

4. Think about the deepest peace you've ever felt. Can you recognize God's presence in the situation?

5. Do you consider surrender to God a victory or defeat? Are you ready for Him to use you in mighty ways?

Conclusion

Now that you know the 10 truths . . . what will do
with them?

When my daughter was in first grade, she reached a mile-stone: she mastered the monkey bars on her school playground.

When I picked her up that afternoon, she jumped in the car with a huge grin. She was so proud of herself, and so was I. As she shared details of her accomplishment, revealing how scared she was because she didn't think she could do it, I realized the life applications.

In kindergarten, she couldn't make it past the second monkey bar. She got so frustrated she quit trying. But as her first-grade friends began mastering the bars, her interest was rekindled. Watching them have fun inspired her to give the bars another shot.

Before she started, she looked to the end of the monkey bars.

Noticing the distance made her sick to her stomach. "When you're not doing it, you're just thinking about it, and that's when you get scared," she told me. But as she pushed through that fear, she grabbed the first bar. Then she grabbed the second bar. This is where her self-doubt kicked in because she'd never made it to the third bar before.

Once again, she looked ahead to the end of the monkey bars. Once again, her fear returned.

"Then I realized something I never did before," she told me, "that I need to try my best instead of giving up and dropping." It took a big burst of courage, but she stretched out her arm and reached for the third monkey bar—and made it!

Overcoming this obstacle was the turning point. With her fear gone, she swung to the end, propelled by sudden confidence. She kept thinking, *I can't believe I just did that! I can't believe I just did that! I CAN'T BELIEVE I JUST DID THAT!*

From that third monkey bar on, she had a great time. She spent the rest of recess doing the bars over and over again.

Far too often in life, we let fear hold us back. Like my daughter stuck at the second monkey bar, we venture no further than what feels safe. We look too far ahead, counting the obstacles between us and our goal, and get sick to our stomach. And as our self-doubt kicks in, past failures come to mind. We want to quit already because we think we've reached our limit.

But through Christ, all things are possible (Philippians 4:13). And when we push through fear with strength from *Him,* we find a freedom in serving God that is exhilarating and life-changing. We look back and can't believe what we accomplished. As we reach the end of one goal, we want another run. Because now that we know the feeling of being propelled out of our comfort zone and into God's territory, we're hooked.

Keep in mind that the joy of serving God often comes *after* an obstacle is conquered. It is obstacles, after all, that build your Christian muscles and strengthen you for next time. So when you're stuck at the second monkey bar, tested in a moment of weakness, don't expect elation. The elation comes once you *survive* the moment and look back with a sense of accomplishment.

I didn't think I could stand the awkwardness of being the one person not drinking at the tailgate party . . . but I did it!

I didn't think I could face the school bully . . . but I spoke up!

I didn't think I could keep from falling for my ex-boyfriend's charms as he tried to use me again . . . but I stood firm!

Your greatest power lies in the small choices you make each day. Whether you choose the world's way or God's way makes all the difference in the kind of life you'll have.

A life that serves God serves *you* well too. It leads you to the water your soul is thirsting for. You'll still make mistakes sometimes. You'll still fall off the monkey bars and have to start over. But the beauty of God is that He's a God of grace and second chances. His power is made perfect in weakness (2 Corinthians 12:9). Despite your flaws and limitations, He wants to use you. And through Christ working in you, you can reach your hand out with confidence and stretch beyond your limits.

So open up your heart and mind to God's will. Listen for His call. Use the 10 Ultimate Truths as guideposts to live an intentional Christian life, remembering what we covered on these relevant issues:

1. Popularity
2. Confidence
3. Reputation
4. Interacting with boys
5. Self-worship
6. Perseverance
7. Patience
8. Image
9. Inner beauty
10. Self-talk

Jesus exists in the present. So when you get scared on life's monkey bars, don't measure the distance to the end, because that overwhelms you. Don't dwell on your past failures, because that discourages you. Instead, focus on the bar in front of you. Think about the one choice you're called to make *right now*. Get through this hurdle before thinking about the next one. And when you encounter a moment of weakness, draw strength from God and what you know is right.

As you live for Him, you'll encourage others. They'll see your joy and peace and want that too. Like my daughter watching her friends ace the monkey bars, they'll be inspired to take a chance. They'll face their fears once again, tapping into a newfound courage.

Come together with girls in faith and share the 10 Ultimate Truths. As iron sharpens iron, you will sharpen each other (Proverbs 27:17). What will result is a better you, a better them, and a better world at large.

There is freedom on the other side of fear and hope on other side of doubt. One great run with God is enough to get you hooked. Trust me on this. I promise it's the truth.

Notes

1. *The Wizard of Oz*, directed by Victor Fleming (1939, Metro-Goldwyn-Mayer Studios).
2. Paul Brian Campbell, SJ, "Wisdom Story—125," People for Others (blog), October 26, 2012, accessed May 23, 2014, http://peopleforothers.loyolapress.com/2012/10/wisdom-story-12-2/.
3. You can learn about Donna Greene's Community Ministry for Girls, Inc., on her website, http://cmfg-inc.org/index.html.
4. Ben Brumfield, "Selfie Named Word of the Year for 2013," CNN Living, November 20, 2013, accessed April 27, 2014, http://www.cnn.com/2013/11/19/living/selfie-word-of-the-year/.
5. InspireMeChannel. (2010, October 17). *The Man and the Butterfly—Inspirational Story about Life*, InspireMeChannel, October 17, 2010, accessed April 27, 2014, http://www.youtube.com/watch?v=EoGkm8GlEpo.
6. Shaunti Feldhahn and Lisa A. Rice, *For Young Women Only* (Colorado Springs, CO: Multnomah Publishers, 2006), 85–103.

Acknowledgments

The best blessings in my life have always been the people in it. I'd like to take this opportunity to thank those who made this book possible.

To Stephanie Holcomb, a counselor at Liberty Park Junior High School. Little did I know when you invited me to speak to your girls, I'd write a blog post from the speech that would ultimately lead to this book. God works in amazing ways, and when He works through a friend, the reward is sweeter. Thank you for setting in motion a dream come true.

To readers of my blog and newspaper column, as well as my Facebook community: a huge *thank-you* for supporting and sharing my work. Connecting with you has been a highlight of my writing journey, and with every uplifting word you offer, I find the courage to dig deeper. Thank you for believing in me and helping me discover my voice.

To Andrew Wolgemuth, my incredible agent, whose expertise, clarity, and skillful guidance allows me to focus on writing. Thank you for being my advocate and advisor. Thank you for jumping in and handling any task, big or small, with timeliness and integrity. It's an honor to be part of your team.

To Margaret and Jack Kubiszyn, my sister-in-law and brother, whose moral support, counsel, and legal services always go above and beyond. Thank you for being there for me and my family. I love you both.

To Rebecca Warren, my gifted editor at Thomas Nelson, whose wisdom, guidance, and market knowledge took this book to a new level. Personally and professionally, I'm inspired by your perspective. Thank you for your endless patience and support. I'm blessed to work with you!

To Michelle Burke, for bringing my blog post to the Thomas Nelson team, and to the amazing individuals at Thomas Nelson who brought this book to life: Laura Minchew, MacKenzie Howard, Katie Powell, AnnJanette Toth, DJ Lipscomb, Hannah Zehring, Kristen Baird, and Gabe Wicks. To be backed by such a talented, hard-working, and enthusiastic team is priceless, and I'm grateful for each one of you.

To Father Bob Sullivan and Father John McDonald of St. Francis Xavier Catholic Church, for cultivating my spiritual growth. Your ability to convey God's truths in relevant, real-life terms impacts my writing, and in our church community, my anxious soul finds love, hope, rest, and renewal.

To Donna Greene, a role model for me. Watching how you

engage with young women, support their dreams, and build them up has shown me how to respect and love tomorrow's leaders, mothers, and world-changers. Thank you for devoting your life to the next generation. Thank you for showing me how it's done.

To Jennifer Cray and Dan Starnes, for giving me a platform in the pages of *Village Living* and *280 Living*, and to my community of Mountain Brook, Alabama, the village that helps me raise my children, grow in faith, and find my way as a wife, mother, friend, and neighbor.

To Jeannie Cunnion, a writing friendship that has influenced me profoundly. On a night when I was lost and stuck, you had answers, and for that I'm so grateful. Thank you for helping me live in faith and deepening my desire for Jesus. In the comfort of your words, I'm touched by God's grace.

To my first readers, the prayer warriors and special ladies who reviewed my manuscript to help me improve it: Krissie Allen, Kimberly Powell, Mary Frances Graves, Julie Stewart, Katie Houser, Mary Alice Fann, and Ridley Fann. Thank you for taking time out of your busy lives to help me. I'm grateful for each of you.

To my girlfriends, old and new, far away and near. Thank you for softening the edges of a hard world. Thank you for revealing to me, through every stage of life, the joys of sisterhood, the healing power of laughter, and the bonds that unite all women.

To my sisters and sisters-in-law: Krissie Allen, Dana Wolter, Mary Kathryn Gerkin, Margaret Kubiszyn, Elene Giattina, and

Renee McMinn. How lucky am I to count you as *family*? To be related to so many smart, talented, kind, fun, and good-hearted women is a gift. You have shaped who I am and always show up for me. Thank you for your love and loyalty. I love you all.

To Becky and Bubba Kampakis, my devoted in-laws, who raised my husband to love and respect women, which now shines through as he raises four daughters. You were right, Papou; when you get married, you marry family. I knew the Greeks were a loving group, but joining the Kampakis family exceeded my expectations. Thank you for the great times and memories. Thank you for embracing me as a daughter. I love you both.

To my parents, Lucy and Jack Kubiszyn, whose voices of love and encouragement play in my head daily. What I didn't notice growing up is what I appreciate most now: how you centered our family on God, pointed us to the truth, and drew me out of my shell with unwavering support and affirmation. This book reflects the childhood you gave me. Thank you for building me up. I love you both so much.

To my daughters, Ella, Sophie, Marie Claire, and Camille. You girls are my heart and soul. Life before you was the dress rehearsal that prepared me for the real thing, that moment I'd realize, "This is it. *This* is life." As I raise you, I'm growing up too. I've becoming more of the person God designed me to be.

Ella, your empathy, kindness, and cheerful spirit enlighten me. You build bridges, not walls, and that draws people in. Always keep your positive outlook. Continue seeing what's good, right, and true. Keep spreading love and peace because our dark and broken world needs your light and hope. God has equipped you and your sisters for great things, and I can't wait to see what's ahead.

Sophie, I envy your fearlessness. I wish I had your strength, energy, and passion for people. When I'm with you I feel stronger and braver, and that is your gift—empowering others beyond their comfort zone. Always keep your compassion and fierce loyalty to friends. Nurture your heart for God and continue leading others to Him.

Marie Claire, I owe my writing career to you, because during your pregnancy I quit *talking* about writing and actually *started* writing. More importantly, you're my cuddle bug, a happy-go-lucky girl who radiates love, warmth, and joy. I marvel at how God works through you in your profound statements and contagious laughter. Stay on course as a self-starter and let God continue using your gifts to grow His kingdom.

Camille, you're the baby, the fourth child I didn't think we needed because our family seemed complete with three children. But God's plans were bigger and better, and for that I'm eternally thankful. You draw our family closer, because in our common love for you, we bond. Always keep your optimism, sense of humor, and enthusiasm. Chase after God the way you chase your sisters, and He'll use you in mighty ways.

And to Harry, whose name should appear on the cover of this book as co-author. Whenever someone asks, "How do you write with four kids?" I answer, "I have a great husband. It wouldn't be possible without him." My mom was right; you *are* the best thing that ever happened to me. Thank you for being my safe place, my sounding board, my home base. I love you beyond words.

And to Christ my Savior. While I wish I'd spent my entire life seeking Your reality instead of the world's, I'm thankful You can bring good from my mistakes and misguided experiences. Thank You for Your mercy and promise of salvation. Thank You for covering me when I fall, for Your power is made perfect in weakness (2 Corinthians 12:9). To God be the honor and glory.